12 PILLARS

of a Healthy Church

Be a Life-Giving Church and
Center for Missionary Formation

Waldo J. Werning

St. Charles, IL 60174
1-800-253-4276

Published by ChurchSmart Resources

We are an evangelical Christian publisher committed to producing excellent products at affordable prices to help church leaders accomplish effective ministry in the areas of Church planting, Church growth, Church renewal and Leadership development.

For a free catalog of our resources call 1-800-253-4276.

PRINTED IN U.S.A.

Cover design by: Julie Becker

Second Edition
© copyright 2001
by Waldo J. Werning

ISBN: 1-889638-27-7

TABLE OF CONTENTS

FOREWORD

The church world is in transition. Methods that used to be effective don't work any longer. Those who direct the work of the church are looking for answers and direction in the work of the church. Mainline churches and independent churches are having difficulty in ministry. Old formulas that were tried and tested over the years don't work any longer. Because people put faith in these formulas, their faith in church work is shaken. Many people see their church declining in vitality and faith, but the vital signs that shake them most are the decline in membership and money.

What can we do?

People are searching everywhere for answers to church ministry. Some are looking to pragmatism, trying to find those methods that work. They claim that if the church doesn't have money and members, it doesn't have any ministry. So they're looking for workable techniques.

Others are retreating to the past, some to ancient liturgy; others are returning to hymnology of a church one hundred years ago. They've given up trying to be relevant to the modern world, and they don't seem to care whether or not they reach the world.

Others seek to guide their ministry by polls and surveys. They want to know what neighbors think, so that they can adapt ministry to the needs of their surrounding clientele. At other times they read the surveys from George Barna or the Gallup Polls, trying to be contemporary in their methodology, looking for the latest cutting edge tool.

Still others are studying the "Boomers" or "Busters," trying to formulate a ministry that will reach the new emerging needs of a new emerging generation. Whether they use seeker-services, praise-music worship, multimedia, or even web-page ministries.

Waldo Werning has given us a new vision for church growth. He wants us to look at the Scriptures for our marching orders. When correctly applied, Werning believes the Scriptures are both relevant and workable. He has built this book on the popular volume *Natural Church Development*, by Christian Schwarz, who tells us to look for natural, biotic, and organic growth. The eight principles of natural church growth each make up a chapter, pointing the reader back to the biblical reason for growth.

Beyond this, Werning visits his earlier book *God Says Move*, to discuss four leading indicators of a healthy church. His premise is that healthy churches grow, just like healthy babies, healthy animals, and healthy plants; when they are healthy, they will grow.

The wonderful thing about this book is its resources. Werning doesn't just explain the Scriptures; he has a worktext approach whereby he takes the readers into Scripture, asks a question, and asks them to write out their answers. But even beyond the Scriptures, the worktext approach introduces the readers to many resources for church growth. Werning is not threatened by including other strong resources, and he takes the reader to some of the great church growth experts and their resources to give a sound foundation for growth.

This book has a broad basis for church growth, based on a broad vision for the church. For those who do not understand vision or have no vision, this book will give you a biblical vision. If your vision is already based on Scripture, it will broaden your vision. Just as pillars hold up a building, these twelve pillars will hold up the church and allow it to grow.

Dr. Elmer Towns, Dean – School of Religion

Liberty University – Lynchburg, Virginia

12 Pillars of a Healthy Church

INTRODUCTION

What will your church be in five or ten years? Seriously, will it be a Life-giving Church or a Religious/Christian Museum? Will your church be a depository of institutional/traditionalist/liturgical forms visited by loyal consumers who want their style of ancient spiritual experiences – or will your church communicate the saving Gospel and pure Word of God in words, forms and styles which non-believing neighbors can understand, embrace and join your Life-giving Church?

"I believe the Church in America has no more than five years – perhaps even less – to turn itself around and begin to affect the culture, rather than be affected by it," writes George Barna. "Because our culture completely reinvents itself every three to five years, and people are intensely seeking spiritual direction, and our central moral and spiritual trends are engulfed in a downward spiral, we have no more than a half-decade to turn things around." Barna continues, "Before we can hope to do so, though, we must rekindle our passion for God, recapture a sense of urgency about ministry, and respond strategically to the challenges before us. If the Church does not quickly realign its heart, mind and soul, and consequently redirect its efforts, we will lose our waning platform of influence in American society and people will consistently pursue the path of least moral resistance."[1]

If you are a pastor or leader of a congregation who is seeking to build a truly Life-Giving Church, one which empowers and mobilizes God's people for mission, you will find a simple, integrated, wholistic, Biblical approach in these pages. Here is a spiritual system/model for small and large congregations which helps connect your people to God, to one another, and to a lost world!

This book takes you beyond information and inspiration to application! You are given the knowledge, resources and tools to implement an expanding spiritual model to equip leaders of your church to disciple members for their ministries. It proposes the base for a growing system that discovers, trains, and mobilizes an expanding group of leaders and an exploding number of members. Here are the principles of the Acts 14:21-25 Church growing out of Eph. 4:11-16 and 2 Tim. 2:2 principles. The goal is to build your congregation as a Life-Giving Church and Center for Missionary Formation.

Healthy Church Initiative

If you are a leader who desires to have a healthier church, you will discover valuable resources in **12 Pillars of A Healthy Church**, together with the companion publications, **Natural Church Development** (by Christian Schwarz), and **God Says Move**. They reveal the eight quality characteristics and four leading indicators of a healthy church.

Christian Schwarz' research in over 1,000 congregations in 32 countries uncovered what many of us, who have been consultants to churches for many years, have observed in many congregations. Schwarz discovered that the Healthy Church Initiative is a totally different concept or approach.

By empirical research, Schwarz discovered what we saw and learned by many years of field experience. He identified two distinct and different spiritual characters/cultures in churches – the technocratic/institutional church and the Biblical/natural/biotic church. The unquestioned use of traditions and technology tends to shape our perspective of the church as an institution or organization to be maintained rather than building the body of Christ. Two columns show how there are two distinct and different spiritual characters/cultures in churches:

Institutional Church	Biblical Church
NEEDS	EDUCATE (WORD)
Tell (Bible study lectures)	Teach (Interactive Bible study)
Church Support (Behavioral Christianity)	Spiritual Formation (Spirituality)
Group's Goals	God's Goals
Maintenance	Mission Outreach
Reactive	Proactive
Fruits	Roots
Traditional/Organizational Model	New Testament Model
Pastor/Staff Service (Spectator Christianity)	Members' Service (Priesthood of Believers)
Law-Centered (Legalisms, rituals)	Grace-Centered (Law and Gospel)
Program-Giving	Life-Giving
Mobilize Without Empowering	Empower and Mobilize

Telling that "the ship must be turned around," George Barna writes, "Before we leave the port, though, we must be reminded of our fundamentals – namely, the foundational elements that limit, direct, and shape our ministry purposes and efforts."[2] Indeed, we must seriously study and consider the character and nature of the church - it's DNA, as Bill Easum suggested in his presentation at a conference.[3] The DNA of the church is seen in the definition of its character and nature – the Church of the Lord Jesus

Christ. The problem is both theological and practical, as seen in the doctrine and practice of the church. Barna states the case clearly, "Always seek the truth and act upon it strategically."[4]

The mission of the church is defined by its DNA in the Great Commission. The church DNA is to make disciples who make more disciples. The description of the DNA of the church is to be seen in its Mission Statement, which is the action the church takes. The church is to live out its DNA in all that it does. The DNA is to be expressed in a Mission Statement that clarifies territory, strategies, and opportunities. Building a healthy church means that the DNA establishes vision, develops core values, helps people discover their spiritual gifts, and encourages and motivates them to use those gifts.

Being faithful to the church DNA means that theology and belief must be applied in compelling ways. Christians are to act on the principles they profess. This book raises a challenge to church leaders to take seriously the church DNA (Gospel character and nature), and represent Christ faithfully. The basic nature of the church is displayed through the use of the 12 pillars, which will guide you to structure your church to be a Life-Giving Church and a Center for Missionary Formation. The DNA and purpose of the church is to empower and mobilize God's people to accomplish the tasks they are called to do. The document – the Bible – reveals the DNA that is to be expressed in the life of the church. Our DNA reminds us that the church should be what God has called it to be.

In practical terms, Christian Schwarz, in **Natural Church Development**, tells us the church is to be natural, biotic, and organic, not technocratic, which focuses on organization and methods. This is a serious call, as George Barna states, "That goes beyond the debate about the need for change; it is a strategic plan for the rebirthing of the Christian faith...It is an urgent plea for the people of God to stop dabbling in religion and to grow in spiritual maturity...This is a call for us to stop playing Church and start being the Church by demonstrating the transformation that has occurred within us as a result of an absolute, paramount commitment to Jesus Christ."[5]

Churches and leaders are being tested to prove that they are what they claim to be, and that they are a true representation of Jesus Christ. Now, instead of being reactive to our circumstances, we act on our DNA. Our actions need to be directed on the basis of the nature of Christ's church.

The Healthy Church Initiative Includes
Being a Center for Missionary Formation

The first known congregation to organize as a Center for Missionary Formation was First Evangelical Lutheran Church of Les Cayes, Haiti, whose pastor is Rev. Israel Izidor (whom this author discipled/mentored at the Fort Wayne Seminary and in Haiti). Adopting the Acts 14:21-25, Eph.

4:11-16, and 2 Tim. 2:2 models, by God's grace, Rev. Israel Izidor, in a little more than five years, has seen God build about 80 churches and missions with 8,000 worshipping weekly, and 38 schools with about 7,500 students. The principles of the Center for Missionary Formation have been shared in Haiti, South Africa, and recently in India, as well as congregations which have field-tested the materials of the "Empowering and Mobilizing God's People" Discipling Series.

Robert Frost tells about the man who came to two roads in the woods, and he took the road less traveled – and that made the difference. Scott Peck's book, The Road Less Traveled, offers the thesis that change is necessary if we are to grow and mature. Change takes us away from the place we have been, and takes us somewhere we have never been before. Not everyone wants to take that route. They prefer not to change but stay on the familiar road and, as a result, they are not healthy and do not grow. Hence, the road of Biblical change is all too frequently "the road less traveled." But that road is the one that makes a difference.

The road I propose does not require us to be confrontational, but act tenderly with quiet determination to proclaim, teach, mentor, and set an example for leaders and members alike of what it means to be a Life-giving Church. These dynamics of spiritual growth will ultimately lead to effective organizational and functional change without conflict. It ignites explosive growth to empower and mobilize God's people for their ministry and mission. Wherever necessary, we call for a change from a technocratic to an organic body of Christ church – expressing its DNA. It takes more than techniques to grow a healthy church. We need to know who we are and act upon that fact.

12 Pillars of A Healthy Church will help pastors and leaders to cultivate health in their church. You see how church health is quantifiable by seeking to have 12 strong pillars in your church. When leaders focus on health to this extent, God's grace will help them grow.

Quality Ministry Tools

12 Pillars of A Healthy Church reveals quality ministry tools for building a healthy church as a Life-giving Church and Center for Missionary Formation. The Discipling/Stewardship Center offers the "tough-minded" mission handbook, **God Says Move, Go Where He Leads**, while ChurchSmart Resources offers **Natural Church Development** with its standard of eight quality characteristics of a healthy church, as the basic resources for the Healthy Church Initiative to be established in your congregation. Many other helpful and important materials for strengthening your congregation in the twelve pillars are proposed. It all adds up to an excellent mix of Biblical principles and practices based on Acts 14:21-25.

There are various leaders today who basically are pursuing their own good version of this model, and they are traveling the "road less traveled." Each is challenged to have their own custom-built model. Wherever you are in your search for a model that fits your church, I pray that these proposals will stimulate you to gain clearer and deeper insights, and encourage you to develop your model more perfectly.

CHAPTER ONE

God Says Move – Go Where He Leads!

C hapter One of *God Says Move – Go Where He Leads!*, one of the two other basic resources for building a Life-giving Church and Center for Missionary Formation, begins with this statement: "God's mission requires mapping and moving for effective ministry and mission." Chapter Two tells how we can "move from maintenance to mission." If you believe the church is God's instrument for missionizing the world, then you will want to study that book for the what and why of workable hands-on ways to revitalize the church. It reveals the "moves" that can dynamically impact the vitality of your church.

If you believe that God, by His Spirit, has imparted into the life of every church the spiritual dynamic to grow into a healthy, vital body, you will find **Natural Church Development** an important resource for building a strong Life-giving Church. It supplies insights into discovering God's principles for building the church and removing any obstacles that might prevent the release of the spiritual dynamic for growth. It does not offer programs or models to manufacture growth within the church. The author, Christian Schwarz, uses the illustration of a barrel with eight staves to symbolize the importance of the eight quality characteristics of a healthy church. The barrel can only hold water to the height of the lowest stave. So he argues, a church can only grow as much as its "minimum factor," which is the lowest of the eight quality characteristics in their church. He challenges churches to resist the temptation to work on improving areas in which they already excel while ignoring their minimum factors, for by doing this, they do not increase their minimum factor nor their church health.

While **Natural Church Development** outlines the eight quality characteristics of a healthy church, **God Says Move** gives emphasis to these qualities and adds four more leading indicators – making 12 pillars by which congregations are to be evaluated as Life-Giving Churches and Centers for Missionary Formation.

The reading, discussion, and planning for the process proposed by these two books will allow you to custom-build your changing and growing model, as you proclaim and teach the Life-giving Word, and disciple and mentor leaders who, in turn, disciple and mentor the members. You will be mapping a more vigorous future to do "God's work in God's way," as J.

Hudson Taylor says, and you will "gain God's supply."

Effective mapping will lead to aggressive moving in God's direction – where He leads. God's Word leads to God's work in God's time. This is not a synthetic building of church growth, but a natural church development growing out of the Life-giving Word of God. This will assure that your church is a church in mission with leaders in motion.

A New Equation/Framework

When is a congregation a healthy church? Christian A. Schwarz and his research staff came to conclusions which are a tremendous help for church leaders to assess and revitalize their congregations. The results are published in the book, **Natural Church Development**, which is a work that could "liberate thousands of pastors from debilitating mythologies that have plagued their daily lives. It could give them hope, direction, and finally full confidence their work is pleasing to God," says Bill Hull. Traditional thinking and practice are sometimes merely myths.

As the twelve quality characteristics and leading indicators unfold and are fully exposed, you will see that they grow out of Biblical texts – Acts 14:21-25, Eph. 4:1, 7, 11-16, and 2 Tim. 2. It is a dynamic way for mapping the future and moving the congregation in the way God desires.

As I read **Natural Church Development** by Schwarz, and as I wrote the book **God Says Move**, I recognized once again how the context of ministry and mission has changed, whether I know it or not or whether I like it or not. A dramatic cultural change reveals the fact that "reality isn't what it used to be," as Walter Truett Anderson said. A new reality of communication, culture, and relationships now exists which the church must understand if it is to reach effectively its own members and the non-believers in the community. Our ministry in the 21st Century must take seriously the cultural changes around us.

John Maxwell says that breakthroughs/changes happen at three times:

1. When leaders hurt enough that they are eager to;

2. When they learn enough that they want to; and

3. When they receive enough that they are able to.

Breakthrough leaders and change are critical to any church that is to remain true to its New Testament roots, and to have its modern-day practice of the 1st Century model. This means a move from tactics to an integrated strategy, as methods are adapted in the context of components of a larger, comprehensive strategy. The Biblical change agent will always ask the question, "What similarity does our present practice have with the substance of the 1st Century church?"

Let Christ Control, and the Holy Spirit Change the Church

Sometimes traditions, personal pride and power, control and shout louder than the spiritual needs of the people and the call of our Savior to win the lost. It is easy for leaders to have dull ears to people who are crying out for Christian community, and are speaking the truth in love. Some listen only to older voices which speak only for the traditions of the church. Thus, they lose the very people who believe the Christian message and true cause of the institution. Breakthrough leaders and change agents do not seek to win their own way but rather, if need be, lose a battle of control for the sake of winning the war.

One thing does not change: Biblical truths and Christian doctrines! The thing that a healthy church can and will change is its style of communication and methods. Through the Holy Spirit by the Word, the church must constantly be "re-formed" and transformed in its practice. It must be washed clean of the traditional barnacles that may attach themselves to the congregation, which come out of culture and human habits. Far more is involved than a shift from hymnbooks to praise choruses. Nor will the church be renewed by one-day retreats or a church council/board of directors resolution. Rather, it necessitates a complete overhaul of our understandings and attitudes of what it means to be Christian and to be the church. As Steven Covey says, we first must understand before we can hope to be understood.

"Traditionalists" whistle into the winds of change, insisting that everyone accept a single, absolute style or form from the past, and often maintain that this is the way to preserve Biblical truth. Often, the result is cultural Christianity or a local form of legalism. Those who desire Biblical church renewal not only take seriously their responsibility for absolute truth, passionate spirituality, Christian character, a witnessing faith, a Christ-like attitude and building Christian community, but they will also take seriously a removal of barriers. They will adopt styles and forms which do not obscure or muddle the New Testament model.

Who dares to continue to carry on business as usual in the face of dramatic cultural transformation or to assume that the people to whom we preach and teach today have the same spiritual concerns or are raised in the same religious context to whom we ministered in the 1950's and 1960's, or our fathers did in Europe in 1850. Will we avoid wasting time and energy on styles of worship, teaching and ministry that no longer meet spiritual needs or reach the ears of the people? A congregation can be irrelevant to such an extent that it reaches no one but its members, and does not retain many of its children.

Research by George Barna tells us that only one-fourth of American people strongly agree that "the Christian churches in my area are relevant in the way I live today."[6] This means that people are distinguishing between Christian faith and the church as an institution, between religion and spirituality. Irrelevancy in communication and programs and methods results in people saying that church is boring and that worship is a humdrum repetition of the same old rituals week after week. Too many churches have confused the primary obligations of the church with the secondary means by which it accomplishes these tasks. Those churches apparently neglect their Biblical charter. They ignore their own weaknesses, and even corruption. They offer empty rituals, not meaningful Biblical worship. They reflect culture instead of Biblical truths that transform lives.

Traditional churches can become healthy churches. Healthy churches can become healthier. Can we envision new ways to carry out the Biblical truths of God's grace and Christ's love to a world that refuses to accept any single truth as absolute? By the Spirit's power, church leaders can revitalize and enhance some of the forms or styles of spirituality in which most of us were raised. Any church can become a Life-giving church, by God's grace, if it wants to and asks God to make it happen.

Life Systems

As God created the human body with an integrated life system of the digestive, pulmonary, arterial, nervous and other systems for the health and survival of the body, so the body of Christ/Christian community through the local church should embrace the twelve core values of the spiritual life model to be a healthy church. These twelve basic pillars are the life or process that grows out of a Word and Sacrament ministry.

Dan Reeves developed and uses ten critical points as his LifeSystemsTM approach to strategic planning and congregational revitalization, which includes spiritual disciplines, mobilization, mentoring, people flow strategies, and organizational streamlines. Reeves proposes a number of parts of the church LifeSystemTM which are similar to a number of the quality characteristics of a healthy church. His perspective asks for a comprehensive shift from a clergy-centered ministry approach to releasing and empowering lay leaders and ministry teams. He criticizes controlled agendas which stifle ministry.

Reeves offers his own new equation/framework for building a healthy church, and challenges churches to restructure and revitalize their established styles, structures and strategies. The 12 pillars of a healthy church, as the 10 points of the LifeSystemsTM, are interacting with each quality characteristic/pillar and increase capacity for ministry impact. As the individual parts/pillars get stronger in their own functions, the whole church is growing healthier. Church health comes from the interaction of the multiple pillars/characteristics. The parts or pillars of the life system do not impose set programs in the congregation, but focus on producing conditions where the church can be healthy to insure that maximum potential is reached. Thus, the real needs of the congregation are addressed to gain maximum fruitfulness.

Can we gain a new equation/framework? This is what the Lord says: "Forget what happened in the past, and do not dwell on events from long ago. I am going to do something new. It is already happening. Don't you recognize it? I will clear a way in the desert" (Is 43:18-19). The Lord said to the workers to lead the chosen people to a victorious life: "Don't be afraid, my servant, Jacob, Jeshurun, whom I have chosen" (Is 44:2).

God is on the Move

Can you see that God is on the move in America and throughout the world through churches that seek to be obedient to Christ's Great Commission and faithful to God's infallible Word? God is doing a new thing. "God is birthing a new church," writes Robert N. Nash, Jr..[7] Loren Mead says that "we are...midwives for a new church working to help our present forms and structures to give birth to forms appropriate for the new mission of the church."[8]

Will we be eager participants in the birth of new communication modes, forms and structures which convey faithfully ancient Biblical truths and principles? Will we have the patience of working two to five years to reach our full stride in gaining strength in all 12 pillars of a healthy church?

Will we take the road which truly makes a difference? Or, will we be among those who travel the traditional and much traveled road of the institutional/technocratic church? The road less traveled will lead us to become a healthy church as we adopt the New Testament model. Regardless of culture, the Life-giving Church will offer the truth of God's grace and Christ's love to its culture, enhance the spiritual lives of its members, and provide a place of community that accurately reflects the Gospel of Christ and the kingdom of God.

An in-depth study of the difference between the institutional church and the Biblical church is presented in **God Says Move**, pps. 28-39. This also provides a history of how we came into the rut of traditionalism. Many cannot find the spiritual vitality which feeds them adequately. "Spirituality" is not what some traditional churches believe it to be – performance of certain kinds of ceremonies, programs and activities. Churches need to be willing to face the reality of their own spiritual inadequacies or weaknesses.

A healthy church will not allow the practice of its community and spirituality to mirror the prevailing culture, or reinforce the values of society. Such churches are a type of club which offers an American way to be religious, emphasizing cultural values, but soon become trapped in those ways so that they offer little else. Some of these have a very strong orthodox doctrine, but their communication and style confuse or turn off their audience to the extent that the message is not heard. In the process, the church loses its distinctiveness and flavor, and weakens its community, not being "salt" of the earth. Being Biblically based while using different kinds of methods and styles need not be incompatible. Increasingly, people will look past them whenever they seek meaningful and helpful spiritual communities.

Another drag on the church is dependence on committees and programs. Leonard Sweet writes, "A church dense with committees is a regatta of red tape that stands for unspiritual commitments, wasted time, unproductive hours, poor stewardship, and bored scribbling on the back of envelopes."[9] In place of committees, healthy churches form ministry teams and small ad-hoc groups which are created as a need arises and then dissolved once the need is met. The organic approach to ministry is the foundation principle which is proposed in Schwarz' book, **Natural Church Development**.

Acts 14:21-25

God Says Move, pps. 196-197, reveals the outline of an Acts 14:21-25 church. This is a model of the church with four parts or activities: evangelize the lost, build the believers, organize for outreach through leadership development, and plant churches. Each part or activity has an educational component: V.21, evangelizing the lost requires that seekers and new converts learn the basic doctrines of the Christian faith through a Bible study course, and that every member is a missionary; V.22, believers are to be built in faith through Bible study courses which fulfill the requirements of Eph. 4:12 to empower and mobilize God's people, with the goal that every member is a Bible student; V.23, organizing for outreach requires selecting and training leaders who are committed to the Lord and to growth as they participate in intensive leadership development, making the church a Center for Missionary Formation and a Life-giving Church; Vs. 24-25, challenges the congregation to plant new churches, moving into new territories.

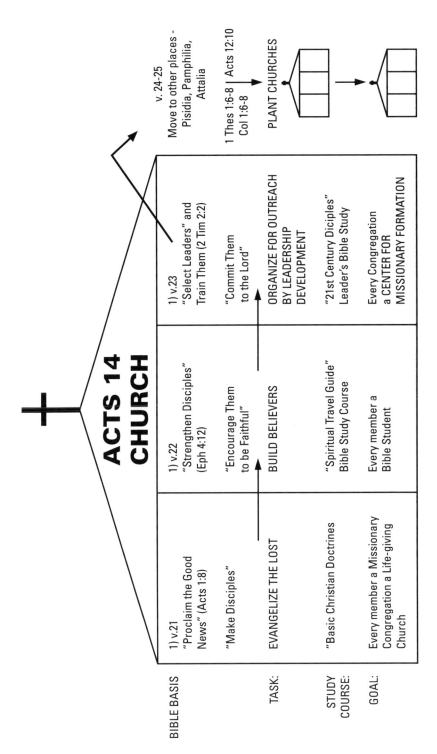

ACTS 14 CHURCH

	1) v.21	1) v.22	1) v.23
BIBLE BASIS	"Proclaim the Good News" (Acts 1:8)	"Strengthen Disciples" (Eph 4:12)	"Select Leaders" and Train Them (2 Tim 2:2)
	"Make Disciples"	"Encourage Them to be Faithful"	"Commit Them to the Lord"
TASK:	EVANGELIZE THE LOST	BUILD BELIEVERS	ORGANIZE FOR OUTREACH BY LEADERSHIP DEVELOPMENT
STUDY COURSE:	"Basic Christian Doctrines"	"Spiritual Travel Guide" Bible Study Course	"21st Century Diciples" Leader's Bible Study
GOAL:	Every member a Missionary Congregation a Life-giving Church	Every member a Bible Student	Every Congregation a CENTER FOR MISSIONARY FORMATION

v. 24-25
Move to other places -
Pisidia, Pamphilia,
Attalia

1 Thes 1:6-8 | Acts 12:10
Col 1:6-8

PLANT CHURCHES

Ephesians 4:1, 7, 11-16

God Says Move, pps. 129-132, shows Eph. 4 to be a New Testament model for the church. V.1 urges all Christians to live worthy of the call which they have received from God, both in their daily lives and in their ministering in and through the church. V.7 tells that each one of us has been given grace as Christ gave it out, and have been gifted to serve and to minister. V.11 reveals that God has given pastors and teachers as spiritual leaders to require them to "prepare God's people, to serve," which is accomplished through intensive Bible study. God's system here consists of membership development through life-long Bible study. How long should this continue? "This is to continue until all of us are united in our faith and in our knowledge about God's Son, until we all become mature, until we measure up to Christ, who is the standard" (V. 13). V. 15 exhibits how spiritual growth happens: "Instead, as we lovingly speak the truth, we will grow up completely in our relationship to Christ, who is the head." The deployment of every believer to minister according to the gifts received is discovered in the simple divine plan in which each believer ministers to others: V. 16, "He makes the whole body fit together and unites it through the support of every joint. As each and every part does its job, He makes the body grow so that it builds itself up in love." When each one functions faithfully according to his or her call and gifts, the Body grows and builds itself up in love.

The Eph. 4 plan or divine blueprint for believers operating effectively by God's grace is the answer to segmented and fractured programs by bits and pieces of exhortations for people to support church maintenance plans.

Disciple-making should be the center of all church activities. Spiritual multiplication and reproduction of believers, not just adding members to the church, was the approach of Jesus and Paul. Jesus said, "Go and make disciples...teaching them to do everything that I have commanded you" (Matt 28:19-20). Paul said, "We should stop going over the elementary truths about Christ and move on to topics for more mature people" (Heb. 6:1a).

The Eph. 4 "Empowering and Mobilizing God's People" model activates the entire church by equipping believers through an intensive educational curriculum to erergize the priesthood of all believers in the most Biblical and practical way. Members are fed and led by God's Word to be totally obedient to Christ's Great Commission. Interactive educational resources are available to open doors to mobilize Christians to enter many new avenues of Gospel ministry. Believers are empowered to initiate, lead, and become engaged in the comprehensive, extensive, and all-embracing work which Christ has given them in His Church. The laity are empowered to be full participants, not merely spectators or bystanders.

2 Timothy 2:2 Discipling Model

God Says Move, pps. 249-250, tells of the New Testament approach for reaching all people through Christian nurture for leadership development. The key text is 2 Tim 2:2, "You've heard my message, and it's been confirmed by many witnesses. Entrust this message to faithful individuals who will be competent to teach others." This process of disciple-making for developing teachers and leaders is the basic approach on which all other church life should revolve. Believing that the maturing of disciples is a vital part of the Great Commission, we will determine by God's grace to develop believers who are strong enough to multiply themselves spiritually through others.

"Empowering Leadership," which is the heart of the 2 Tim 2:2 principle and approach, makes teachers/facilitators responsible to guide the participants/students toward self-discovery and group-discovery for maximum learning and putting their faith into practice through interactive learning. This suggests that congregations are to be Equipping Centers, making the training and empowering of all leaders and believers a priority. All believers are to be released for full participation in God's mission through becoming teachers, spiritual leaders, care-givers, support group directors, and personal witnesses of Jesus Christ. The goal of interactive Bible studies is to follow 2 Tim 2:2 and Eph 4 is to make every congregation a Center for Missionary Formation, which offers educational resources for making men in mission, women in mission, youth in mission, children in mission – beginning with pastors in mission. That is the basis for churches in mission.

Life-giving Churches

As you seek quality in church life, you will be helped in this as you read or re-read Rick Warren's **The Purpose Driven Church**.[10] You will do well to take time to read **The Lay-Driven Church**, by Melvin J. Steinbron, which outlines spiritual care-giving by lay people in the congregation. Steinbron asks four key questions:

"1. Are people ready to give and receive this ministry?

2. Are pastors ready to give this ministry to their people?

3. Are people ready to do this ministry?

4. What kind of structure does this ministry take?"[11]

Steinbron refers to the "Lay Pastors' Ministry," a congregational care by lay people. Because this may confuse people with the pastoral role, I prefer to name it "Lay Shepherding Ministry" or "Lay Spiritual Care and Ministry."

Steinbron offers additional refreshing insights on how to be a healthy church.

Reality Check

1. How close is your church character and practice to its Biblical DNA? (10 is highest)

   Tradition-Centered   **Biblical DNA**

   1   2   3   4   5   6   7   8   9   10

   Talk about your answer.

2. Please evaluate your congregation on the basis of the following measurement.

   Program-Giving Church   **Life-Giving Church**

   1   2   3   4   5   6   7   8   9   10

   Talk about your answer.

3. Please evaluate your congregation as a Center for Missionary Formation on the basis of the following measurement.

   Few in Bible Study/Training   **Center for Missionary Formation**

   1   2   3   4   5   6   7   8   9   10

   Talk about your answer.

CHAPTER TWO

Eight Quality Characteristics and Four Leading Indicators of a Healthy Church

Through careful research, Christian Schwarz has verified the link between church health and spiritual growth in his book, **Natural Church Development**. Robert E. Logan writes in the Preface, "The research results confirm what many leaders have known intuitively – that healthy churches are growing churches, making more and better disciples in loving obedience to Christ."[12] Refusing to focus on numbers and quantity, and rejecting technocratic thinking, Schwarz discourages work in our own strengths, but encourages dependence upon God and the spiritual principles which He incorporated into His Church.

Schwarz' book offers four building blocks, consisting of content (what should we do?), timing (when should we do it?), method (how should we do it?), and background (why should we do it?). These first four parts answer the four basic questions of church renewal and spiritual growth, while part five addresses the how of practically implementing these building blocks of natural church development in ten action steps. We are urged to avoid methods which are insufficient, because they are inconsistent with God's plan. This book is based upon a different approach for church renewal, for it is "natural" or "biotic" church development. This means nothing less than the use of the principles of life by letting God's growth automatisms flourish, instead of wasting energy on human-made programs or technocratic strategies.

Besides the eight quality characteristics, I have added four leading indicators, which are also basic to Biblical church renewal, and which I have found vital and relevant to church health through my 49 years of consultations with churches throughout the United States and 16 countries overseas. This results in a balance of inreach and outreach. What is offered here is the model which is being taught to pastors and lay leaders who are mentored through the Five-Year Renewal Process, "Catch the Vision of His Mission," in the India Evangelical Lutheran Church. This is also being shared with churches in the United States.

What is being provided in my book (growing out of principles found in **Natural Church Development** and God Says Move) is the fact that local congregations are living organisms, created and designed by God to grow and reproduce by His grace. Such a church is positioned to engage in ministry that births new life. To revitalize a congregation, God first transforms the lives of the pastor and church leaders, who create the new strategies to produce more and stronger disciples. This is a church/ecclesiastical life system of twelve core values based upon our Biblical belief.

The pastor and congregation will benefit by scheduling a series of 12 sermons and Bible studies based on each of the 12 pillars of a healthy church. This resource, **The Healthy Church – Sermons and Bible Studies**, is available from Concordia University, 2811 NE Holman Street, Portland OR 97211-6099 (Ph) 503-288-9371.

Quality Characteristic/Pillar #1

EMPOWERING LEADERSHIP
(Eph 4:7, 12-16; 2 Tim 2:2)

"God's favor has been given to each of us. It was measured out to us by Christ who gave it....Their purpose is to prepare God's people, to serve, and to build up the body of Christ. This is to continue until all of us are united in our faith and in our knowledge about God's Son, until we become mature, until we measure up to Christ, who is the standard. Then we will no longer be little children, tossed and carried about by all kinds of teachings that change like the wind. We will no longer be influenced by people who use cunning and clever strategies to lead us astray. Instead, as we lovingly speak the truth, we will grow up completely in our relationship to Christ, who is the head. He makes the whole body fit together and unites it through the support of every joint. As each and every part does its job, the body grows so that it builds itself up in love" (Eph 4:7, 12-16).

"You've heard my message, and it's been confirmed by many witnesses. Entrust this message to faithful individuals who will be competent to teach others" (2 Tim 2:2).

Most churches have failed to show the importance of leadership, especially empowering leadership, and do not adequately identify, nurture, and support those who are elected or appointed to lead. Relatively few leaders have been prepared for their responsibilities.

Leadership requires that leaders pose a compelling vision of the future that the church with its members should pursue. Leaders are responsible to motivate people to embrace and live according to their individual commitment as Christians and corporate commitment as the church. Thus, the church is to find and empower people whom God has called for the task of leadership.

Congregations are to plan for intentional leadership development and the exercise of leadership gifts. Pastors are expected to enlist and mentor leaders to obtain the spiritual potential God has given them so that leaders can equip, support, motivate and mentor believers, enabling them to become all God wants them to be. Through intensive Bible study, members are mobilized for expanded service/ministry to the extent that leaders and workers are trained and equipped for their tasks. Empowerment of leaders is foundational in the life of a healthy church. Leaders as mentors empower men and women. Mentoring is key to feeding and nurturing believers for spiritual growth.

As a mentor, the leader is an equipper for ministry rather than simply a doer. Thus, it is important to spend time training someone for ministry than to do it oneself. The enormity of Christ's mission challenges every leader to have someone in training - to be a mentor.

Empowering is a key adjective is a vital part of the task of leadership. It is helping people do what they are called to do, and gives people responsibility to use their gifts and to gain desired results. Empowerment is different than delegation, which is helping people do what we want them to do. Empowerment gives them the tools, the right, and the opportunity to use their God-given gifts as God leads through the church.

Empowerment means to equip, to educate, to train, and then to release for ministry. It happens especially through interactive Bible studies, which requires participants to do homework and share their answers in class. Thus, God prepares leaders and positions them. The size of the task is not as important as the fact that God has sized them for their role. Interactive Bible studies present the practical application of Eph. 4 in the areas of leadership and membership development to pursue God's call for greater ministry and mission. It is a life-long learning process for spiritual growth and discovery, which leads from knowledge and understanding to action. Beginning with information, it takes the participants to spiritual formation and transformation – a living relationship with a living God and fellow believers.

Dwight D. Eisenhower once said, "Leadership is the ability to get a person to do what you want him to do, when you want it done, in a way you want it done, because he wants to do it."

Strong leadership with passion for God's purpose is essential to help people learn their potential by discovering their gifts and using them. Faithful leaders lead with love, and have a clear vision of the mission. They recognize and solve growth-restrictive problems and make the right decision at the right time. As they cultivate and maintain good relationships with the members, leaders make them productive and fruitful. Quality and excellence in the church goes from the top down. A leader is, first of all, a servant, not an authority figure in the church bureaucracy. Paul was a model of servant leadership:

Melvin J. Steinbron writes of Paul, as leader, "He was a father without being paternalistic. He was an apostle without being dictatorial. He was a leader without being domineering. He was an authority without being authoritarian. He was an example without being proud. He was an equal without abdicating his authority. He corrected without controlling. He taught without demagoguery. He advised without being officious. He persuaded without manipulation. He exhorted without vindictiveness. He compromised without sacrificing his convictions. He suffered without self-pity. He adapted without losing integrity. He saw himself as a servant; we see him a master. He saw himself a sinner; we see him a saint. He saw himself the least apostle; we see him the greatest."[13]

Leaders who think themselves inadequate should consider the attitude of Moses and how God dealt with him. Moses discovered a very important lesson on leadership from his father-in-law, Jethro (Ex 18:13-26). Moses learned (Exodus 3-4) that his claim of inadequacy and resistance to God's call was not acceptable to God, when he said, "Who am I that I should go...? They will never believe me or listen to me!...I speak slowly, and I become tongue-tied easily...Please, Lord, send someone else." God called Moses to journey with His people and bring them to where God wanted them. Moses' task was to teach them God's decrees and laws and the duties they were to perform. He was to select, appoint and train people who fear God. Leaders need to bring difficult cases to Moses. They were to minister to others. Moses learned that he was not to keep the leadership to himself, but it was to be shared.

Jethro revealed to Moses his condition: "What you're doing is not good...This is too much work for you. You can't do it alone!"

Jethro gave him the solution: "You must be the people's representative to God and bring their disagreements to Him. You must instruct them in the laws and the teachings, show them how to live, and tell them what to do. But choose capable men from all the people, men who fear God, men you can trust, men who hate corruption...They should bring all important cases to you, but they should settle all minor cases themselves."

Jethro then told him of the benefits: "Make it easier for yourself by letting them help you...You will be able to continue your work, and all these people will have their disagreements settled so that they can go home." Many pastors will recognize the need to understand and solve the problem, determine the solution, and then enjoy the benefits.

A congregation cannot grow past the ability of the pastor and leaders to care for the people, for the spiritual care through leaders and lay people has an impact upon its capacity and energy to grow.

Many people in many congregations who are called leaders are little more than "workers" in the church. A worker is a believer who does a task or ministry work. A leader is one who is faithful and able in serving others, and leads, mentors, oversees, and delegates work to individuals or groups. Leaders are responsible to God for the character and service of a church or a ministry.

Leaders hold a position of authority, while workers hold a position of influence. Leaders are responsible to give an account to God for the flock, while workers for their own lives. Leaders establish policy, while workers help implement it. Leaders equip others to do the work of ministry, while workers share in that work.

The main role of leadership is to teach and mentor. Mentoring relationships develop two dimensions: personal development (becoming) and ministry development (doing). This helps the one being mentored to get God's perspective of what God is doing and wants to do in their lives. It assists them in determining God's will for their lives, as they reflect and refocus themselves according to God's plan. 2 Tim 2:2 provides the classic example of educating Christians for maturity (**God Says Move**, pp. 187-193). The Apostle Paul told Pastor Timothy that the Word of God which he had heard from him (Paul) was to be taught to reliable/faithful individuals who would be able to teach others also. This is the divine system for leadership development! Teachers are to be multiplied for the nurturing of all members. This is an educational model for leadership development that has been neglected by many pastors and churches.

Leadership development involves four levels of spiritual development: 1) being evangelized, which ends when faith in Jesus is established by the Holy Spirit; 2) being grounded or established in the faith, which involves ordinary Bible study; 3) being nurtured for maturity, which is accomplished by interactive, self-discovery and group-discovery Bible study approaches, and applicational and relational Bible courses; 4) being a discipler/teacher/mentor. The fourth level is where spiritual multiplication and reproduction of leaders and through leaders is taking place – building disciples.

In order to introduce the **Healthy Church Initiative** to the congregation, church leaders should schedule 12 weeks of sermons and Bible studies, using the resource, **The Healthy Church — Sermons and Bible Studies**, available from Concordia University, 2811 NE Holman Street, Portland, OR 97211-6099 (Ph) 503-288-9371.

Additional material: Study "Quality Characteristic 1: Empowering Leadership," pps. 22-23 of **Natural Church Development**.

Reality Check

How do you rate your congregation on "Empowering Leadership" at this time?
What are the strengths?
What are the weaknesses?
Do leaders function as servants?
Do they focus on consensus building?
How are members being trained for church staff and ministry positions?
Are all staff members multiplying themselves through lay-leader development?
Are all leaders and officers active in Bible study/classes?
How many have received leaders' training courses?
Are annual or semi-annual Leaders' Retreats conducted?
What new steps do you propose to take?

EMPOWERING LEADERSHIP RESOURCES
Primary Resources

1. Train all leaders and potential leaders through the 26-week interactive Bible study leader's course, **21st Century Disciples with a 1st Century Faith** (Fairway Press-Discipling/Stewardship Center). It

should be a goal of each Life-giving Church to require all leaders and teachers to complete this course or an equivalent one. This training for spiritual growth should have priority over skills training. A pastor in Michigan reported that, after study of the **21st Century Disciples** course, 19 of the 20 participants became "highly visible, aggressive leaders" in the congregation.

2. **Empowering Leaders Through Coaching**, by Steven L. Ogne and Thomas P. Nebel, Manual and Logbook (ChurchSmart Resources). The Manual helps leaders do a better job in coaching others to reach their full potential in life and ministry. It is a blueprint for successful coaching and mentoring leaders so they finish well.

3. **Raising Leaders for the Harvest**, by Robert E. Logan and Neil Cole (ChurchSmart Resources), introduces the concept of Leadership Farm Systems, an organic process of leadership development with results in natural and spontaneous multiplication of disciples, groups, ministries and churches.

Secondary Resources

1. **Developing the Leader Within You**, by John Maxwell (Nelson).

2. **Developing the Leaders Around You**, by John Maxwell (Nelson).

3. **The Making of a Leader**, by J. Robert Clinton (NavPress).

4. **Leaders on Leadership**, by George Barna (Regal).

Minimum Level Activity

1. Study Characteristic 1: "Empowering Leadership," pps. 22-23 of **Natural Church Development**.

2. Study the book, **12 Pillars of a Healthy Church**, with your church leaders.

3. Read **Natural Church Development** and **God Says Move–Go Where He Leads**. Use these books with your leaders.

4. Expect teachers and leaders to participate in the leadership development program and be regular in Bible study and small groups. Set a goal when all leaders are expected to have leadership training and be active in Bible classes.

5. Invite all teachers, elders, officers, and leaders to enroll in the **21st Century Disciples With A 1st Century Faith** interactive Bible study course (or equivalent) for leaders.

6. Enlist qualified leaders as facilitators in the interactive Bible study small groups.

7. Conduct regular Leaders' Retreats.

Moderate Level Activity

8. Read **Raising Leaders for the Harvest**, by Bob Logan and Neil Cole.

9. Use Quality Characteristic 1; **Implementation Guide to Natural Church Development**.

Maximum Level Activity

10. Train leaders through **Empowering Leaders Through Coaching**, by Steven L. Ogne and Thomas P. Nebel, with a Manual and Logbook (ChurchSmart Resources).

11. Read one of the secondary resource books, **Developing the Leader Within You, Developing the Leaders Around You, The Making of a Leader,** or **Leaders on Leadership.**

Quality Characteristic/Pillar #2

GIFT-ORIENTED SERVICE/MINISTRY
(Eph 4:7; 1 Pet 4:10-11)

"God's favor has been given to each of us. It was measured out to us by Christ who gave it" (Eph 4:7).

"Each of you as a good manager must use the gift that God has given you to serve others. Whoever speaks must speak God's words. Whoever serves must serve with the strength God supplies so that in every way God receives glory through Jesus Christ. Glory and power belong to Jesus Christ forever and ever! Amen" (1 Pet 4:10-11).

Christ is not only the source and standard for ministry in the church, but He also gives the gifts which make this ministry possible. Before there is service, there are gifts, which Christ has made available to believers (Eph 4:7). All Christians are given gifts for ministry. These gifts usually correspond to the abilities of individuals. As supernatural endowments of the Holy Spirit, these are grace-gifts bestowed by the Lord on believers for use in the church.

Whatever the believer has been given, there is no cause for boasting nor basis for pride. "Who says that you are any better than other people? What do you have that wasn't given to you? If you were given what you have, why are you bragging as if it weren't a gift?" (1 Cor 4:7).

Peter summarizes these grace-gifts to be used in a speaking ministry and a helping ministry (1 Pet 4:10-11) – the ministry of the Word and the ministry of service. Believers are to be "good managers of God's gifts." The exercise of the grace-gifts is for the "common good" (1 Cor 12:7), and "for one another." Gifts are given not for selfish enjoyment, but for the edification of the whole Christian community. Whatever the gifts, they are to be used (Rom 12:6).

Healthy churches should assist Christians to serve in their area of giftedness, functioning more in the power of the Holy Spirit, and less in their own strength.

Christ's church with all members is a "royal priesthood" (1 Pet 2:9). There is only one order of priests (laos, "the people of God"). All are called as ministers/priests, but all are not pastors, nor elders, nor deacons, nor leaders. Our High Priest, Jesus, made all Christians priests for God and ministers to others.

The spiritual gifts of the priesthood of all believers will be identified and developed in order to serve as functional servants of Jesus Christ. Ordinary people accomplish extraordinary work through use of gifts Christ has given them.

The church and its members are to work on the basis of spiritual gifts. Paul declared, "Brothers and sisters, I don't want there to be any misunderstanding concerning spiritual gifts" (1 Cor 12:1). Many believers do not think of themselves as being called by God to serve with the gifts Christ has given them.

"You didn't choose me, but I chose you" (John 15:16). We are to accept spiritual giftedness and Christ's call as essential to our life in the church to do our work as ministers of God. The use of spiritual gifts is basic for the quality of ministry of the church. It is our task to discover, develop and use them.

Additional Material: Read Quality Characteristic #2: Gift-Oriented Ministry (pp.24-25, Christian A. Schwarz, **Natural Church Development**).

Reality Check

How do you rate your congregation on "Gift-Oriented Service/Ministry" at this time? What are the strengths? What are the weaknesses? What new steps do you propose to take? Are new believers integrated actively?

GIFTS-ORIENTED SERVICE/MINISTRY RESOURCES

GRASP Spiritual Gifts for Christian Ministry and Service

Part of a lay ministry package, "Getting a GRASP on your personal mission," GRASP helps church members to learn God's purpose and call in their lives.

G-groundings – Christian beliefs and values which guide us to our purpose.
R-role – services and activities in which you excel.
A-abilities – what you enjoy, what comes natural.
S-spiritual gifts – discover and use spiritual gifts (Eph. 4:7).
P-passion – with a heart on fire, serve God with your gifts.

GRASP is a Spiritual Gifts tool to assist members to identify their unique gifts, callings and passion. By applying Jesus' words to daily living, they will find meaning and their purpose, discerning God's call for life, finding the skills and resources they possess.

MOUNTAIN MOVERS INTERNTAIONAL, 4000 Midway Road, Suite 303, Carrollton TX 75007 214-435-0753 *Whamit@aol.com* Website: Mountainmovers.org

Minimum Level Activity

1. Read Characteristic 2: "Gift-oriented Ministry," of **Natural Church Development**, pps. 24-25.

2. Use GRASP inventory which fits the beliefs of your church, and encourage all members to discover and identify their grace-gifts and use them.

3. Use Characteristic 2; **Implementation Guide to Natural Church Development**.

Quality Characteristic/Pillar #3

PASSIONATE SPIRITUALITY
(Eph 5:15-16; 6:10, 18; Col 3:1-17; Gal 5:22-26;
James 3:17; 2 Peter 1:6-9)

"So then, be very careful how you live. Don't live like foolish people but like wise people. Make the most of your opportunities because these are evil days" (Eph 5:15-16).

"Finally, receive your power from the Lord and from His mighty strength....Pray in the Spirit in every situation. Use every kind of prayer and request there is. For the same reason be alert. Use every kind of effort and make every kind of request for all of God's people" (Eph 6:10,18).

"Since you were brought back to life with Christ, focus on the things that are above – where Christ holds the highest position. Keep your mind on things above, not on worldly things. You have died, and your life is hidden with Christ in God. When Christ your life appears, then you, too, will appear with Him in glory. Therefore, put to death whatever is worldly in you: your sexual sin, perversion, passion, lust, and greed (which is the same thing as worshipping wealth). It is because of these sins that God's anger comes on those who refuse to obey Him. You used to live that kind of sinful life. Also get rid of your anger, hot tempers, hatred, cursing, obscene language, and all similar sins. Don't lie to each other. You've gotten rid of the person you used to be and the life you used to live. And you've become a new person. This new person is continually renewed in knowledge to be like its Creator. Where this happens, there is no Greek or Jew, circumcised or uncircumcised, barbarian, uncivilized person, slave, or free person. Instead, Christ is everything and in everything. As holy people whom God has chosen and loved, be sympathetic, kind, humble, gentle, and patient. Put up with each other, and forgive each other if anyone has a complaint. Forgive as the Lord forgave you. Above all, be loving. This ties everything together perfectly. Also, let Christ's peace control you. God has called you into this peace by bringing you into one body. Be thankful. Let Christ's word with all its wisdom and richness live in you. Use psalms, hymns, and spiritual songs to teach and instruct yourselves about God's kindness. Sing to God in your hearts. Everything you say or do should be done in the name of the Lord Jesus, giving thanks to God the Father through Him" (Col 3:1-17).

"But the spiritual nature produces love, joy, peace, patience, kindness, goodness, faithfulness, gentleness, and self-control. There are no laws against things like that. Those who belong to Christ Jesus have crucified their corrupt nature along with its passions and desires. If we live by our spiritual nature, then our lives need to conform to our spiritual nature. We can't allow ourselves to act arrogantly and to provoke or envy each other" (Gal 5:22-26).

"However, the wisdom that comes from above is first of all pure. Then it is peaceful, gentle, obedient, filled with mercy and good deeds, impartial, and sincere" (James 3:17).

"To knowledge add self-control; to self-control add endurance; to endurance add godliness; to godliness add Christian affection; and to Christian affection add love. If you have these qualities and they are increasing, it demonstrates that your knowledge about our Lord Jesus Christ is living and productive. If these qualities aren't present in your life, you're short-sighted and have forgotten that you were cleansed from your past sins" (2 Peter 1:6-9).

Most Christians need a more rigorous plan of spiritual exercise than we offer them. A spiritual coldness of members in churches presents a danger, as they sometimes concentrate on ritual in place of relationships, and the form of worship replaces the practice of worship. Instead of being on a mission for God, they just exist. They need to go to the Great Physician for a touch of His healing Power.

We believe that only the presence and power of the Holy Spirit can enable Christians to live transformed lives, experiencing God and being obedient to Him. By God's grace, they are to practice their faith with joy and enthusiasm for Christ and His mission.

Christian character and values are the basis of passionate spirituality which results in what we do. We do what we value. Passionate spirituality is the spiritual principle on which our life is to be built. Life finds meaning by loving and serving God. Repentance and forgiveness is vital to removal of barriers to greater spirituality.

Questions people might ask themselves: What is your spiritual goal for today and for the future? For your family? What is your professional or business hope? What about health and wellness? What about finances? What is your vision for growing stronger spiritually? What is your plan for service to God? For your community? For your recreation and relaxation? What would you do if you could not fail?

God Says Move (pp. 75-117) refers to basic issues in order to be faithful to God's call to be sanctified and live a holy life. **God Says Move** (pp. 180-187) emphasizes prayer and spiritual warfare related to passionate spirituality. Passionate spirituality begins with intense prayer, asking the Spirit to empower and guide, not only following Jesus as the Truth but also as the Way and Life. Congregational life will include prayer chains, intercessory prayer lists, prayer vigils and a conscious effort to make prayer an ever-present ingredient in every phase of congregational life.

Many people are frustrated in their Christian experience, because they know God has more in store for their lives than what they have now. Many want to be touched spiritually and meet God relevantly, but do not know how it happens. Their passion will be aroused when they are with leaders and members who are passionate. Competent leaders are needed who have the kind of passion that generates passionate followers. We seek a passion for things that matter to God. Nothing is more powerful than when God's people, led by a spirit-filled leader, come together with passion around the God who they truly understand to be awesome and loving.

Bible study courses suggested in the **Primary Resources** and in the **Secondary Resources** are designed to help you as a believer to:

- Hear when God is speaking to you;
- Clearly identify the activity of God in your life;
- Believe Him to be and do everything He promises;
- Love Him with all your heart, mind, strength, and soul;
- Praise Him so that your life can be constantly filled with His joy;
- Commune with Him in prayer so that you are constantly aware of His presence;
- Adjust the direction that He is taking your life and what He wants to do through you;
- Know what you should do in response to His Word you are studying;
- Experience God working through you in a way that only God can;
- Die with Him so that you can live forever – with Him!
  Through these Bible studies and others that are available, leaders can help believers to discover their purpose in life and how God wants to use them, and experience God on the basis of such Biblical realities as:
- God pursues a real and personal relationship with you by His love;
- God speaks by the Holy Spirit through His Word, prayer, circumstances, and other Christians to reveal Himself, His purposes, and His ways;
- Sometimes your service in response to God's call may lead to a crisis of belief that requires faith and action, always depending on the Holy Spirit;
- By God's grace, every hindrance from life must be removed through repentance and forgiveness, making major adjustments in life wherever necessary;
- You must place yourself absolutely at God's disposal;
- Learn how to prevail through fervent prayer;
- Know God by experience and obey Him as He accomplishes His work through you.

Philip Spener's program for spiritual renewal provides some helpful insights: He called for Christians to study the Scriptures in small groups; he urged the restoration of the priesthood of all believers; he asserted that Christianity does not only consist in knowing but also in action that comes from a loving heart; he proposed that the emphasis of spiritual training (including pastoral) should be on spiritual formation; he called for a revolution in preaching and teaching which concentrated on spiritual growth, not just on church work to be done.

The healthy church provides training, models and resources for members of all ages to develop their daily spiritual disciplines. The healthy church does not allow its members to view transformation in Christ as a one-time event, or even a solution to a "crisis" rather than a lifelong "spiritual process." The healthy church leads all members to a purpose-driven life, preparing them to fight the good fight of faith.

Here is a prayer for passionate spirituality: Lord, grant me clarity of mind, purity of heart, sincerity of purpose, tenacity of will, and trust in Your grace and power to make me Your obedient servant and witness through Christ!

Additional Material: Read Quality Characteristic #3: Passionate Spirituality (pp. 26-27, Christian A. Schwarz, **Natural Church Development**).

Reality Check

How do you rate your congregation on offering "Passionate Spirituality" at this time? What are the strengths? What are the weaknesses? What Biblical teachings and study courses does your congregation offer to help the members truly experience God and love Him and people passionately? What new steps do you propose to take?

PASSIONATE SPIRITUALITY RESOURCES

Primary Resources

1. **Spiritual Travel Guide**, Waldo J. Werning (Fairway Press-Discipling/Stewardship Center). A 15-week interactive Bible study course for small groups, applying and relating Christian truths to life. This is a very practical review of Christian faith, which helps people to reclaim their faith and be able to share it.

2. *Experiencing God*, by Henry Blackaby and Claude King (Broadman), widely used small group interactive Bible study which has led many to great spiritual growth.

3. *The Purpose-Driven Life*, by Rick Warren – a ten-week series of sermons to help believers discover their purpose, define their life mission and write a personal mission statement, organizing time, doing what's important, etc. (Audio cassette, disk or transcript from The Encouraging Word, P. O. Box 6080-388, Mission Viejo, CA 92690; phone (714) 888-2500; fax (714) 888-2600).

4. *Focused Living Resource Kit*, by Terry Walling (ChurchSmart), helps individuals become intentional in their spiritual development and focused in their living, helping warriors to wage the spiritual battle using spiritual weapons. New strategic focus is obtained by examining their past, clarifying their future, and identifying resources that will facilitate future growth and effectiveness. Includes a leader's guide, six audio cassettes, and three self-discovery workbooks.

Secondary Resources

1. **Spiritual Fitness Exercise**, Waldo J. Werning (Fairway Press-Discipling/Stewardship Center). A 10-week small group study which leads participants to weekly activities of daily devotions, reading a chapter of a provocative book, witnessing, care-giving and tithing. This should be part of a curriculum established by the congregation for the second and third year of discipling members.

2. **Living Without Slaveries**, Waldo J. Werning (Fairway Press-Discipling/Stewardship Center). A 15-week Bible study to help hurting people with addictions, compulsions and obsessions, helping a church organize support groups. This should also be part of the interactive Bible study curriculum for the second and third years of discipling, recruiting especially those who have the ability to be care-givers, and also those who are struggling with addictions, compulsions, and obsessions.

Minimum Level Activity

1. Read Characteristic 3: "Passionate Spirituality," pps. 26-27, **Natural Church Development**.

2. Invite all members to get involved in interactive Bible study, such as **Spiritual Travel Guide** and **Experiencing God**, or equivalent ones which you choose.

Moderate Level Activity

3. Use Characteristic 3, "Passionate Spirituality."

4. Consider preaching the ten-week series of sermons, **The Purpose-Driven Life**, by Rick Warren, editing them for your situation.

5. Plan a curriculum of small groups, using such books as **Spiritual Fitness Exercise** and **Living Without Slaveries**.

Quality Characteristic/Pillar #4

FUNCTIONAL STRUCTURES/ADMINISTRATION/
SERVANT LEADERSHIP
(1 Cor 1:30; 2:4; Eph 1:22; 1 Tim 3:1, 5)

"You are partners with Christ Jesus because of God. Jesus has become our wisdom sent from God, our righteousness, our holiness, and our ransom from sin....I didn't speak my message with persuasive intellectual arguments. I spoke my message with a show of spiritual power" (1 Cor 1:30; 2:4).

"God has put everything under the control of Christ. He has made Christ the head of everything for the good of the church" (Eph 1:22).

"This is a statement that can be trusted: If anyone sets his heart on being a bishop, he desires something excellent" (1 Tim 3:1, 5).

A congregation cannot be healthy if its organization and life is built on faulty foundations or pillars. One of those pillars is having a functional structure and administration. The government of the church has Biblical authority, and is not merely administrative.

George Barna asserts, "Most of our research suggest that the typical church is structured in ways that prevent it from effectively ministering to people. In most cases, the very organizational framework of the congregational church is inappropriate for addressing the needs resident in today's world....The design of the typical local church - which remains the primary model of ministry - sets them (and us) up for defeat....They often confuse structure and methods with theology and message."[14]

Effective and functional structure means that we recognize that unhealthy systems enable problems to continue and even grow. It means that the church builds people before buildings, so that we do not shape our buildings, and then our buildings end up shaping the programs and activities of the church.

As we form and sustain the functional structure, we view the church primarily as a living organism rather than an organization where the structure is developed before fully considering function, ministry and mission.

We seek functional forms and structures so that the body of Christ may perform effectively. We want to avoid barriers of traditionalism and institutionalism, where a change in methods is fiercely rejected and considered disloyal to the past. The intimate connection between structure and life is that nothing in forms/structures/methods must hinder the communication of the saving Gospel of Jesus Christ and the ministries of the congregation to be faithful to the Great Commission. Structures are not unspiritual, but neither are they the essence of the church - but instruments to communicate the Gospel and disciple the people.

Building a functional structure and administration requires less use of boards and committees, and more dependence on ministry teams and adhoc groups which accomplish both short-term and long-term tasks. It demands fluidity and pro-active responses to ministry and mission opportunities for the people to do God's work.

We cannot build the Church without organization, and we must not build the organization without relating it to Christ's Church. The cost of organization is never as great as the lack of it. Since we organize in order to accomplish our purposes, we should have just enough organization to get the work done right. It is harmful to lose sight of proper administration and supervision of the work (1 Cor 12:28; Acts 20:28).

It is very important that we think and talk about vision and ministry in Biblical terms and models, not institutional, organizational or traditional. Going from vision to aggressive ministry requires that leaders offer multiple entry points into the church, and offer multiple opportunities for members to worship, grow, care, and share. The pyramid is build from the bottom, not the top.

This approach is enhanced as leaders are aware of how levels of dissatisfaction are lowered and levels of satisfaction are raised (**God Says Move**, pp. 54-57). Kennon L. Callahan, originator of this idea, shows that the relational characteristics are the source of satisfaction, and that where they are present, the higher the level of satisfaction. He states that the more the functional characteristics (mere programs and activities) exist by themselves without building relationships, the lower the level of satisfaction. It is important to recognize this fact, because there is a constant pull for pastors and leaders to work to put more programs and facilities in place, rather than giving attention to relational aspects and interactive Bible studies for spiritual growth and building people.

Emphasis on functional structures and administration will also help avoid problems in communication by confusing substance and style (**God Says Move**, pp. 57-59). There is always the temptation to change the map by focusing on forms and style, that may confound and dilute the substance, which is the Biblical message.

Healthy churches with functional structures/administration will focus on reviewing, analyzing and check-listing each one of the eight quality characteristics and four leading indicators annually – the 12 pillars of a healthy church. They will closely observe the percentile rating of each one of these categories, and work faithfully on raising those characteristic in which they rate the lowest. ChurchSmart Resources offers quality materials to aid the congregation to do this.

The healthy church seeks to develop and use the kind of facilities, equipment, and systems that will provide maximum support for the growth and development of its ministries. Through empowering of the laity, it will always seek to begin new ministries.

Additional Material: Read Quality Characteristic #4: Functional Structures (pp. 28-29, Christian A. Schwarz, **Natural Church Development**).

Reality Check

How do you rate your congregation on "Functional Structures/ Administration/Servant Leadership" at this time? What are the strengths? What are the weaknesses? What new steps do you propose to take? Do you clearly articulate your purpose and vision? Do the members understand and accept the vision? Is your congregation functioning mechanically or as a spiritual movement?

FUNCTIONAL STRUCTURES/ADMINISTRATION/ SERVANT LEADERSHIP MODEL RESOURCES

Primary Resources

1. Comprehensive materials and resources, and workshops and consultations are provided by ChurchSmart Resources, 3830 Ohio Oave., St. Charles, IL   60174; 1-800-253-4276 e-mail ChurchSmart@compuserve.com. Website: www.Churchsmart.com   Not only do they offer the basic book, **Natural Church Development**, but they also supply the "Natural Church Development Survey," which helps a congregation examine the essential 8 quality characteristics of a healthy church, aiding leaders to discover the greatest weaknesses and strengths. The **Survey** is supplied with a copy for the pastor and 30 for key lay people, which are to be returned to ChurchSmart Resources, who will process them and provide results for $150.

2. Creative Consultation Services, Church Growth Center, P. O. Box 145, Corina, IN   46730-0145 (Phone 800-626-8515; fax 219-281-2167; e-mail creativech@juno.com; website www.churchdoctor.org) offers congregations consultations, creative insights analysis, staffing consultations, etc. An outstanding evaluation form, Church Vitality ProfileTM Questionnaire, designed to reflect the health and potential of your church, is available from this Ministry. Dr. Kent Hunter, Director, offers a valuable book on church growth, Confessions of a Church Growth Enthusiast.

3. Consider membership in the Association of Courageous Churches, 15808 Manchester Road, Ellisville, MO 63011-2208 (888-567-4187; e-mail acc4u@juno.com; website www.acc4u.org), which offers helpful books and resources, including worship, music, leadership skills and stewardship, to equip Christian leaders to develop bold ministries, helping to organize strategies to leverage their strengths. The Association also conducts conferences.

Secondary Resources

1. Church Growth Institute, P. O. Box 7000, Forest, VA 24551 (800-553-4769; fax 804-525-0608; website www.churchgrowth. org) offers

books, resources, and seminars on how God is moving in His church to empower God's people for local church ministry.

2. Lay Renewal Ministries, 3101 Bartold Avenue, St. Louis, MO 63143 (Phone 800-747-0815; fax 314-647-7604) offers motivational workshops designed to provide church leaders with a systematic, Scriptural plan for leading their churches to effectively accomplish God's will.

3. Sonlife Ministries, 526 North Main Street, Elburn, IL 60119 (800-770-4769; fax 630-365-5892; website www.sunlife.com), offers Growing Healthy Churches conferences that propose practical, intensive training that will help implement the key values of Jesus' method of making disciples and equipping believers.

4. Services which help to learn of the LifeSystems™, which relate to the concepts in **12 Pillars of a Healthy Church** are: Congregational Analysis, Congregational Clustering, LifePlanning (in association with Tom Paterson), Team Building, Conflict Resolution. For additional information, contact Dr. R. Daniel Reeves (800-373-5077; fax 805-922-4347; e-mail raspc1@aol.com).

5. Search Institute, Thresher Square West, Suite 210, 700 South Third Street, Minneapolis, MN 55415 (800-888-7828; fax 612-376-8956), offers workshops, publications, and a catalog on planning/visioning and faith development.

6. Net Results (Publisher, Herb Miller), 5001 Avenue N, Lubbock, TX 79412-2993 (800-762-8094), is a publication on leadership, stewardship, and evangelism, and church planting.

7. Read **Team Strategy: How to Structure and Lead the Ephesians 4 Church**, by Larry Gilbert (Church Growth Institute).

Minimum Level Activity

1. Read Characteristic #4: "Functional Structures," pps. 29-29, in **Natural Church Development**.

2. Study **12 Pillars of a Healthy Church** with your leaders.

3. Use the Planning Pyramid with your church leaders in each area of congregational activity (p. 24).

4. Make an analysis of your congregation, using **Your Church Has Personality** by Kent Hunter (Church Growth Center, Corunna, IN).

5. Contact The Church Doctor™ Ministries to consider use of the Church Vitality Profile™ Questionnaire, which is designed to reflect the health and potential of your church.

Maximum Level Activity

6. Read **Team Strategy: How to Structure and Lead the Ephesians 4 Church**, by Larry Gilbert (Church Growth Institute).

Quality Characteristic/Pillar #5

INSPIRING/HIGH IMPACT/GOD-EXALTING WORSHIP SERVICES (Ps 100; John 4:23-24)

"Shout happily to the Lord, all the earth. Serve the Lord cheerfully. Come into His presence with a joyful song. Realize that the Lord alone is God. He made us, and we are His. We are His people and the sheep in His care. Enter His gates with a song of thanksgiving. Come into His court-yards with a song of praise. Give thanks to Him; praise His name. The Lord is good. His mercy endures forever. His faithfulness endures throughout every generation" (Ps 100).

"Indeed, the time is coming, and it is now here, when the true wor-shipers will worship the Father in spirit and truth. The Father is looking for people like that to worship Him. God is a spirit. Those who worship Him must worship in spirit and truth" (John 4:23-24).

Healthy churches seek to have inspiring worship that glorifies God and engages the heart, mind and emotions of the people with God, expressed in a spirit of joy. Vibrant worship resonates in our ears to hear the truths of the Scriptures and songs. Our worship should be Biblically fresh and alive, communicating the pure Word of Law and Gospel, while avoiding code and buzz words or language of another century and another place, which is done at the loss of contact with people and the world that Christ wants to reach.

The only acceptable worship in the Old Testament was when the object of worship was Yahweh, the God of Abraham, Isaac and Jacob. If the object of worship was anything or anyone other than this True God who reveals Himself in the Scriptures, the worship was unacceptable, no matter where, how or when it was done.

In the New Testament, the object of worship is the Triune God, Father, Son and Holy Spirit. If the object of worship is not directed toward this true God revealed in the Word, the worship is unacceptable. Such worship is not limited to a particular time, place, set of formal ceremonies or rituals, but worshipping God in spirit and in truth. Biblical worship in formal gather-ings of God's people requires that the worshipper hear God communicating His good gifts of the Gospel – forgiveness of sins, life and salvation through His Word and Sacraments. The worshipper responds with joy, praise, thanksgiving and obedience. Biblically, the focus is not primarily on the forms of worship, but with the preaching and teaching of the Word of God, as God speaks to His people and they respond in prayers, songs and obedi-ence.

Man is created to worship God out of a loving relationship to Him. Worship is a way of life to glorify God rather than primarily conduct a cer-emony. Corporate worship should be an overflow from God's Word with prayer in relating to God, which results in edifying others and witnessing of the love of God at all times. Worship is meant to sense the awesome presence of God and to build our relationship with Him.

A healthy church gathers regularly as the local expression of the body of Christ, to worship in ways that involve the heart, mind and soul in dialogue with God. Group worship helps us center on the Lordship of Christ, the redemptive work of God the Father through Jesus' sacrifice, and the truths of God's Word, by power of the Holy Spirit.

Worship always takes form, but specific form and worship are not identical. Biblically, true worship which grows faithfully out of the Word is the essential thing. The first concern about form is that it should have Biblical content, and not tied to culture of another people and another age, nor to any other place or style. Forms are only different ways of communicating the truth. If the Biblical content and messages are adequate or similar, there is no deeper or more sincere liturgical form or music, but may be expressed in different cultural expressions and style.

The Bible and Christ our Lord do not impose traditional forms on us for form's sake. Ancient forms and liturgies are not Divine, but are only ones which were written by Saints of the past, or Christ's servants in the present, who have attempted to give us an acceptable Biblical form. Traditions in some instances and, to a certain point, always have value, but when they are raised to the level of doctrine, they are unbiblical. Traditional forms of worship are not to be confused with Biblical doctrine. The Biblical message and truths must be expressed in inspiring/high-impact/God-exalting worship services.

Elmer Towns, in Putting an End to Worship Wars, provides a very helpful resource for concentrating on the content of worship and to see its form and methodology in proper perspective. He does not prescribe forms, but describes the trends and tensions in contemporary churches over worship services. He raises these questions: "What do you do in worship? How do you worship? What motivates you to worship? What are the results of worship?"[15]

Elmer Towns does not write this book to change anyone's worship style, but rather to review it and attempt to do it better. Through study of a number of churches with various worship styles, the author concludes that six worship types exist in America: 1) the Evangelistic Church, which focuses on winning the lost; 2) the Bible Expositional Church, which emphasizes teaching the word of God; 3) the Renewal Church, which focuses on excitement, revival and touching God; 4) the Body-Life Church, which focuses on fellowship, relationships and small groups; 5) the Liturgical Church, which centers on serving and glorifying God through worship and liturgy; and 6) the Congregational Church, which has a balanced approach to worship, expressed by the lay people.

Churches have choices in accepting and developing their own form or forms of worship, but God's Word prescribes the substance of speaking and hearing the Truth, speaking to God in prayer and praise, singing thanks to God for all His mercies in true Christian worship.

Additional Material: Read Quality Characteristic #5: Inspiring/High Impact Worship Services (pp. 30-31, Christian A. Schwarz, **Natural Church Development**).

Reality Check

How do you rate your congregation on "Inspiring/High Impact/God-Exalting Worship Services" at this time? What are the strengths? What are the weaknesses? What new steps do you propose to take? Which of the six worship types does your church practice? Or, do you have a combination of the styles? In the context of your congregation and community, which types/styles should be offered? If so, how?

INSPIRING/HIGH IMPACT
GOD-EXALTING WORSHIP SERVICES
RESOURCES

Minimum Level Activity

1. Read Characteristic 5: "Inspiring Worship Services," pps. 30-31 of **Natural Church Development**.

2. Are all worship services an uplifting spiritual experience in Spirit and Truth?

3. Study **Putting an End to Worship Wars** (Broadman & Holman), by Elmer Towns, with spiritual leaders who are responsible to assist in worship. Then, determine which of the six worship styles is used in your congregation. Are several worship styles or blended services used to meet the needs of all members? What new form or forms should be used to reach all members and your

Moderate Level Activity

4. Use Characteristic 5; **Implementation Guide to Natural Church Development**.

5. For pastors and worship leaders, attend quality seminars or workshops on effective worship, conducted by experienced national or area leaders.

Quality Characteristic/Pillar #6

MULTIPLIED SMALL GROUPS/INTENTIONAL DISCIPLE-MAKING/GROWING IN COMMUNITY (Matt 28:19-20; Rom 14:19, 15:14; Col 3:16; 1 Thess 5:11)

"So wherever you go, make disciples of all nations: Baptize them in the name of the Father, and of the Son, and of the Holy Spirit. Teach them to do everything I have commanded you" (Matt 28:19-20).

"So let's pursue those things which bring peace and which are good for each other" (Rom 14:19).

"I'm convinced, brothers and sisters, that you, too, are filled with goodness. I'm also convinced that you have all the knowledge you need and that you are able to instruct each other" (Rom 15:14).

"Let Christ's word with all its wisdom and richness live in you. Use psalms, hymns, and spiritual songs to teach and instruct yourselves about God's kindness. Sing to God in your hearts" (Col 3:16).

"Therefore, encourage each other and strengthen one another as you are doing" (1 Thess 5:11).

Quality Characteristic #6: Wholistic Small Groups (pp.32-33, Christian A. Schwarz, **Natural Church Development**), the research shows that, even though the interplay of all basic quality characteristics is vital, the one principle that was identified as the most important is the multiplication of small groups.

Jesus gathered a small group around Him, as did Paul. Small groups were an integral part of the life of the church at their time, and in the early centuries. Spiritual growth of people and churches was experienced through Christ-centered small groups.

In informal and formal settings in members' homes, participants can gain Bible knowledge and application to their lives, discuss materials, provide care for people in various needs, and support one another. The benefits of small groups include combining people's energies and abilities, which accomplish more than when they act alone, providing a feeling of belonging as people support people, transforming people's lives, and helping with problem-solving and decision-making. Reasons for small groups are to gain a deeper relationship with God, to find meaning, to be included, to experience community, to give and get care, and to overcome loneliness.

Five essentials of small groups are Bible study, prayer, support, community, and ministry/mission. Groups may be study-oriented, relationship-building, needs-oriented, task-oriented, or a combination of these four categories.

We are committed to build wholistic small groups, which not only study the Bible, but also apply its message to daily life and relate it to others. Wholistic small groups are the natural place for Christians to learn through interactive studies how to build relationships and serve others with their spiritual gifts inside and outside the group. Planned multiplication of small groups or cells is made possible through the continual development of leaders through the implementation of 2 Tim 2:2 and Eph 4:12-16.

Small groups need a solid foundation and basis for measuring their potential and success. Healthy small groups which help people grow spiritually and to serve and minister effectively should have: 1) a clear purpose, with a covenant to which they are committed; 2) a good beginning with leaders who know what it is all about and what to do, and provide positive direction; 3) faithful leaders, who earn the trust of others and are helpful and caring; 4) good communication patterns, which help all participants to understand and learn and want to grow; 5) basic Biblical content, which is applicational and relational; 6) focus on Jesus Christ through the Gospel; 7) growing trust and care among the members of the group; 8) practical ministry and mission beyond themselves; 9) positive decision making, in which all participants work together to apply everything to life; 10) flexibility, which allows for individual and group expression of faith; 11) genuine love that attracts interest and desire for involvement; 12) priority to prayer and the power of the Holy Spirit.

Effective small groups or cells which faithfully provide the Word and love of Christ help the church to be healthy. They help people discover and use their ministry gifts. They equip leadership for the congregation, and provide the ideal setting for members to learn Biblical faith, and trust and minister to each other. They make faith personal. They are the best way to assimilate new members. They give opportunity for people to be involved. Nominal Christians may be drawn by the Holy Spirit to come alive in faith. They provide an opportunity for people to develop their faith, as well as express it.

Effective small groups require careful planning and assessment of the curriculum and instruction. The courses that are to be taught ought to be determined by the purpose and goals. Learning objectives are to be established that will enable those in the small groups to reach the goals. Instruction is best done through interactive studies, in which participants study and write their answers between study sessions, and then share what they have learned.

Leaders should determine materials, time, place and equipment needed to reach the objectives. Effective assessment determines if learning objectives have been met and goals accomplished.

Research and experience have shown that not all the members of any church of small groups will be in small groups. Another form of Bible study, prayer, fellowship, care and support should be provided for them. The goal is that every person and every family is adequately shepherded through personal care.

Reality Check

How do you rate your congregation on "Multiplied Small Groups/Intentional Disciple-Making/Growing in Community" at this time? What are the strengths? What are the weaknesses? What new steps do you propose to take? How many new small groups do you plan to have in one year? In two years?

MULTIPLIED SMALL GROUPS/INTENTIONAL DISCIPLINE-MAKING/GROWING IN COMMUNITY RESOURCES

Primary Resources

1. Read Carl F. George, *9 Keys to Effective Small Group Leadership* (P. O. Box 486, Mansfield, PA 16935: Kingdom Publishers, 800-597-1123).

2. *The Small Group Book: Nurturing Christians and Building Character* L. E. Galloway (Grand Rapids, Michigan: Baker Book House, 1995).

3. It is vital that leaders develop a curriculum of interactive Bible studies for leaders and members which are applicational and relational in nature. Leaders will want to review previously-named interactive Bible studies, *21st Century Disciples with a 1st Century Faith* for leaders (Fairway Press-Discipling/Stewardship Center; *Spiritual Travel Guide* for leaders and members (Fairway Press-Discipling/Stewardship Center); *Experiencing God* (Broadman Press); Spiritual Fitness Exercise (Fairway Press-Discipling /Stewardship Center); and *Living Without Slaveries* (Fairway Press-Discipling/Stewardship Center). Leaders are encouraged both to use other interactive Bible studies of equivalent quality and add to this curriculum.

4. Books, magazines, materials, seminars and resources to learn the keys and acquire the tools for growing small group/cell ministry can be acquired from Touch Outreach Ministries, P. O. Box 19888, Houston, TX 77224-9888 (800-735-5865; fax 281-497-0904). They provide basics and an outline for a comprehensive plan for a dynamic cell structure, and how to multiple life-giving cell groups.

Minimum Level Activity

1. Read Characteristic 6, "Holistic Small Groups," from *Natural Church Development*, pps. 32-33.

2. Organize small groups for special needs: All age groups, parenting, support groups for the hurting, etc. Use the book by Carl George, *9 Keys to Effective Small Group Leadership*.

3. Train the teachers/facilitators through **21st Century Disciples With A 1st Century Faith** course for leaders, or some equivalent course.

4. Build a basic curriculum of interactive Bible studies for small groups for members, such as **Spiritual Travel Guide, Experiencing God, Spiritual Fitness Exercise, Living Without Slaveries**, and other equivalent courses. Plan a major activity of enlisting a maximum number of members in interactive Bible studies, as qualified teachers are prepared to lead small groups.

Moderate Level Activity

5. Use Characteristic 6; **Implementation Guide to Natural Church Development**.

6. Review the ChristCare program of building small groups, and consider training some congregational leaders. Contact Stephen Ministries, 8016 Dale, St. Louis, Missouri 63117-1449.

Maximum Level Activity

7. Plan for your congregation to be a healthy church of small groups ministry.

Quality Characteristic/Pillar #7

WITNESSING/FRUITFUL EVANGELISM/MISSIONS
(Mark 16:15; Acts 14:21; Luke 19:10)

"Then Jesus said to them, 'Go everywhere in the world, and tell everyone the Good News'" (Mark 16:15). "They spread the Good News in that city and won many disciples. Then they went back to the cities of Lystra, Iconium, and Antioch (which is in Pisidia)" (Acts 14:21). "Indeed, the Son of Man has come to seek and to save people who are lost" (Luke 19:10).

Regular mission outreach was a way of life for Jesus, as for Paul. Having been given spiritual food by Jesus, the disciples followed a spiritual exercise of witnessing, as Christ sent them out in personal evangelism. Jesus involved them in a variety of evangelism efforts: personal emphases (sending them out in pairs) – Mark 6:7-13; small groups in homes – Mark 1:29-34, Luke 5:27-32; mass evangelism, sometimes demonstrating God's power through miracles to gain credibility – Matt 14:15-21, 15:32-38.

We are motivated by Christ's love to share the Good News of salvation in our neighborhoods, our nation and our world, regardless of racial, economic or political barriers. We do not depend upon "evangelism programs," but rather on empowering Christians to witness through intensive Bible study and training, recognizing those who have special gifts for witnessing and mobilizing them. Every Christian is challenged to make maximum use of existing contacts through their extended family, friends, coworkers and others. Our ministry and its budget should reflect a high commitment to mentoring for outreach and missions.

A big question about renewal in our congregation is whether we are empowering for local and world evangelism. What will happen tomorrow in mission outreach as a result of what has happened today in Bible study and equipping the saints?

Before Isaiah said, "Here Am I! Send Me!" (Is 6:8), he was lifted by God's glory, as God refreshed him by His presence (Is 6:1, 3), and his nearness to God's holiness led to godly sorrow and repentance, "...I'm doomed. Every word that passes through my lips is sinful. I live among people with sinful lips. I have seen the king, the Lord of armies!" (Is 6:5). An angel took a burning coal off of the altar and touched Isaiah's mouth and said, "This has touched your lips. Your guilt has been taken away, and your sin has been forgiven" (Is 6:7). Then Isaiah was entrusted with God's commission, having his heart and mouth cleansed and ears opened. The same Lord asks you and me, "Whom will I send? Who will go for us?" (v. 8).

Isaiah's blessing of forgiveness while in the presence of God's glory was all about God's purpose for the believers. God has given us the Good News for ongoing evangelism and mission thrusts to emerge. A glorious encounter with God made Isaiah sensitive to God's signals and call. The awesome experience of God's grace should thrust us into the harvest field. We are all sent. The only question is, "Where?"

Mission Activities

The pastor, leaders and members should become increasingly involved in mission and servant activities locally, in our country, and throughout the world. Adults as well as youth are to be enlisted in these evangelism, mission, and service events. Financial ability will dictate how many leaders and members can go beyond local activities and then on to national, and then to international.

Denominations and mission agencies promote and advertise mission and servant events in which leaders and members can be involved.

1. Local Opportunities – Urban ministries and missions are often in need of volunteer work and assistance. Encourage members to become involved in the closest servant event, or with a Habitat for Humanity project.

2. National Opportunities – Denominations and agencies emphasize national mission and servant events for adults and youth.

3. International Opportunities – There are a number of excellent opportunities for mission and servant events fairly close to us - Mexico, Central America, and Haiti. Great opportunities are offered in Russia and China.

   There should be a regular flow of leaders and members going to various places to participate in these mission and servant events.

Additional Material: Read Quality Characteristic #7: Need-Oriented Evangelism, **Natural Church Development**, pp. 34-35, which stresses the need for recruiting and training those who have the gift of evangelism.

Reality Check

How do you rate your congregation on "Witnessing/Fruitful Evangelism Missions" at this time? What are the strengths? What are the weaknesses? What new steps do you propose to take? Do you have a clear understanding of the congregation's culture and the culture of the community? Do you also have a priority on reaching inactive members, those who have dropped out of church, and ones of a different culture? In what mission service and servant events will your pastor and members participate locally, nationally, and internationally?

WITNESSING/FRUITFUL EVANGELISM/ MISSIONS – RESOURCES

Primary Resources

1. Leaders should review and consider the use of **The Way to Life** (Fairway Press-Discipling/Stewardship Center), which provides

seminar training materials, and individual mentoring of members and new believers to share the saving Gospel with others.

Minimum Level Activity

1. Read Characteristic 7: "Need-Oriented Evangelism," pps. 34-35, in **Natural Church Development**.
2. What training are members offered in order to be equipped for articulating their faith in relevant terms
3. Is training and witnessing offered regularly?
4. Are new converts equipped to share their faith with their families, friends, and co-workers?
5. Is mission education promoted so that members are motivated and informed to get involved in the mission of the church?
6. Are members encouraged/challenged to be involved in local servant events, helping congregations in urban areas or wherever there is a need, Habitat for Humanity, etc.?
7. Use **The Way to Life** for equipping members and converts/confirmands to share their faith actively.

Moderate Level Activity

8. Use Characteristic 7: **Need-Oriented Evangelism; Implementation Guide to Natural Church Development.**
9. Encourage/challenge some members to become involved in national opportunities for servant events and mission activities.

Maximum Level Activity

10. Encourage/challenge the pastor, leaders, and qualified leaders to be involved in international servant events and mission activities.

Quality Characteristic/Pillar #8

LOVING RELATIONSHIPS
(John 13:34-35; John 17:23; 1 Cor 13:13, 14:1; 1 John 3:16,18)

"I'm giving you a new commandment: Love each other in the same way that I have loved you. Everyone will know that you are My disciples because of your love for each other" (John 13:34-35).

"I am in them, and you are in Me. So they are completely united. In this way the world knows that You have sent Me and that You have loved them in the same way You have loved Me" (John 17:23).

"These three things remain: faith, hope, and love. But the best one of these is love....Pursue love...." (1 Cor 13:13, 14:1)

"We understand what love is when we realize that Christ gave His life for us. That means we must give our lives for other believers....Dear children, we must show love through actions that are sincere, not through empty words" (1 John 3:16, 18).

Healthy churches offer a loving and helpful Christian community as they challenge members to seek a divinely generated power of genuine, practical Christian love. We do not depend only on verbal communications, but connect and network so that Body-life is experienced by all. People not only hear us talk about love, but also experience it in our contacts with them. Sharing the Gospel is not the fulfillment of dogmatic and moral standards or requirements, but showing love individually and in Christian community as a fruit of faith. Loving relationships produce unity and accountability within the congregation, enabling the church to handle conflict and discipline Biblically and evangelically.

Stephen Ministries[16] is a very important instrument for providing special care for people in special needs, offering caregivers for care receivers. It is the body and community of Christ serving the needs of those who are hurting spiritually, emotionally, physically, materially or who have suffered a great loss. This system attempts to put hurting people in relationship to Christians and the church through caregivers. It seeks to overcome isolation with individuals who need help. The church takes ownership and responsibility for the care and health of members in the congregation. It utilizes the congregation's resources for the good of all as a part of its spiritual immune system.

Stephen Ministries is a system of congregational care that assigns trained care givers to care receivers who are experiencing difficulties and are hurting. Through special training, leaders pursue a prescribed structure and training with materials available only to enrolled churches. The care receiver serves only through the crisis, and then is reassigned. Each Stephen Minister cares for one person at a time. Prescribed training requires over 50 hours.

Stephen Ministry helps generate an atmosphere of loving and caring within the congregation. Care givers are trained for skills in listening, assertiveness, confidentiality, with a professional approach, using Scripture, prayer, personal witness and blessing. The benefit is that pastors are released from overload, and hurting people who would not otherwise be able to be helped receive the care needed in a time of crisis.

Essentials of the **Stephen Ministry** care giver involves listening to people's deepest yearnings, pursuing a system that will meet people's basic spiritual expectation, and empowers gifted people to help people who face crises.

Another ministry which builds loving relationships and identifies needs in a congregation is the **Telecare Ministry**.[17] Members are contacted by telephone once a month for encouragement and actions about any unmet needs and for prayer.

Basic to enjoying loving relationships is the building of a Christian community in the church as the Body of Christ. **God Says Move** (pp. 118-128) offers insights on achieving a healthy Christian community of believers. It encourages fellowship where love is expressed, reconciliation occurs, and everyone experiences love and care.

The healthy church builds loving and caring relationships within families and between members of the church. Christian love requires the context of the whole Body-life of the church. Leaders will identify and develop individuals whom God has called and given the gift of love, and challenge them to be conscious of their servanthood under Christ.

Additional Material: Read Quality Characteristic #8: Loving Relations, **Natural Church Development**, pp. 36-37, which shows how important love and care of all church members is basic to a healthy church.

Reality Check

How do you rate your congregation on "Loving Relationships" at this time? What are the strengths? What are the weaknesses? What new steps do you propose to take? Are small groups developed to help build relationships?

LOVING RELATIONSHIPS – RESOURCES

Minimum Level Activity

1. Read Characteristic 8: Loving Relationships, pps. 36-37, in **Natural Church Development**.

2. Study and consider adopting the **Telecare Ministry**, by which members are contacted once a month for encouragement about unmet needs and for prayer.

3. Make it possible for most members to be active in a small group.

Moderate Level Activity

4. Use Characteristic 8; Implementation Guide to **Natural Church Development**.

5. Consider training for the pastor and several leaders to adopt the **Stephen Ministries** (2045 Interbelt Business Center Dr., St. Louis, MO 63114 ph. 314-428-2600, fax 314-428-7888; e-mail stephen-ministries.org) program in the congregation, providing care-givers for care-receivers.

ADDED TO THESE QUALITY CHARACTERISTICS ARE FOUR LEADING INDICATORS OF SPIRITUAL HEALTH FOR THE CHURCH:

Leading Indicator #1/Pillar #9

CENTRALITY OF GOD'S WORD/GOSPEL/GRACE (2 Tim 3:16-17; Rom 1:16; Titus 2:11-14)

"Every Scripture passage is inspired by God. All of them are useful for teaching, pointing out errors, correcting people, and training them for a life that has God's approval. They equip God's servants so that they are completely prepared to do good things" (2 Tim 3:16-17).

"I'm not ashamed of the Good News. It is God's power to save everyone who believes, Jews first and Greeks as well" (Rom 1:16).

"After all, God's saving kindness has appeared for the benefit of all people. It trains us to avoid ungodly lives filled with worldly desires so that we can live self-controlled, moral, and godly lives in this present world. At the same time we can expect what we hope for—the appearance of the glory of our great God and Savior, Jesus Christ. He gave Himself for us to set us free from every sin and to cleanse us so that we can be His special people who are enthusiastic about doing good things" (Titus 2:11-14).

The preaching and Bible studies of a healthy church must be a proclamation of God's Word that is clear, theologically sound and relevant, so that people might be eager to please and praise God by applying His Word to every area of life out of love for Christ. They live by grace in repentance and forgiveness through the freedom of the Gospel, not by the rules of the law or institutional expectations.

Churches which want to be faithful to their call from Christ to be an authentic New Testament church, will ask the following questions: "Is our agreement concerning the content and centrality of the Gospel (balanced with the Law) true to the Apostolic Word? How shall our church fulfill its prophetic and Great Commission obligation to teach its people and to reach the lost with the pure Gospel? How is the authority of Christ central to everything that we say and do?"

The healthy church will hold a high view of the Bible, the inerrant Word of God, the Sacraments, and of Jesus Christ as the only Savior of the world. The centrality of God's Word/ Gospel/Grace will assure that members do not have a superficial view or understanding of God - God of Justice-God of Love, and the killing power of His Law and the reviving power of His Gospel. There is nothing so sick about a Christian's life or a congregation's existence that a proper use and distinction of the Law and Gospel cannot cure.

The Justifier, Reconciler and Sanctifier is always God Himself, and He has given His full Scripture to make people and the church spiritually healthy. The basic business of the church is to provide the richest supply of the Word of Law and Gospel for every member to gain maximum knowledge, faith, godly living and growth.

God calls for radical spiritual surgery for people who wish to lead a healthy and whole Christian life, which involves repentance and forgiveness in Christ. This means that believers open their lives to God through the Word and Sacraments, recognizing their sins and repenting of them, and accepting forgiveness through Christ.

Forgiveness is the stepping stone to an active Christian life and service. Forgiveness through Christ is the monumental difference in our capacity to be what God called us to be, and to fulfill our eternal destiny. The forgiving Word, given by God both in the Word and Sacraments, is not empty, but a Word that possesses power and strength. God's forgiveness is the transforming grace in Christ.

Resource materials which are relevant to applicational and relational teaching of the Word of God are found in **God Says Move: God of Justice-God of Love** (pp. 65-69); **God Communicates Through the Law and Gospel** (pp. 69-75); **Centrality of Repentance and Forgiveness** (pp. 75-78); **The flow of Grace and Gospel Power for Salvation and Sanctification** (pp. 102-106).

Reality Check

How do you rate your congregation on "Centrality of God's Word/Gospel/Grace" at this time? What are the strengths? What are the weaknesses? What new steps do you propose to take?

CENTRALITY OF GOD'S WORD/GOSPEL/GRACE RESOURCES

Primary Resources

1. **God Says Move** (Ch. 5, pps. 64-84) provides insights into the centrality of God's Word/Gospel/Grace.

2. The intensive interactive Bible studies, **Spiritual Travel Guide** for members, and **21st Century Disciples with a 1st Century Faith** for leaders, are basic resources to achieve the purposes of this basic indicator.

Minimum Level Activity

3. Use the study guides at the end of **God Says Move**, for Bible classes on the subjects of Grace, Law and Gospel, and Repentance and Forgiveness, pps. 64-84.

4. Enlist as many members as possible in the Bible study, ***Spiritual Travel Guide***, which centers on grace, and Law and Gospel.

Moderate Level Activity

5. Offer Biblical courses which deepen understanding and appreciation of the basic doctrines of the Christian faith.

Leading Indicator #2/Pillar #10

MISSION AND VISION-DRIVEN
(Matt 28:19-20; 2 Cor 4:18; John 4:35)

"So wherever you go, make disciples of all nations: Baptize them in the name of the Father, and of the Son, and of the Holy Spirit. Teach them to do everything I have commanded you" (Matt 28:19-20). "We don't look for things that can be seen but for things that can't be seen. Things that can be seen are only temporary. But things that can't be seen last forever" (2 Cor 4:18). "Don't you say, 'In four more months the harvest will be here'? I'm telling you to look and see that the fields are ready to be harvested" (John 4:35).

Do we have a clear sense of God's mission and a compelling vision of the future that is communicated clearly through a master mission strategy and that guides our ministries, personnel, programs, budgets, according to biblical priorities? Do we have a willingness to change and take risks for ongoing effectiveness?

Healthy churches have leaders who become possessed with a cause greater than they are: "For it is God working in you, giving you the will and power to achieve His purposes" (Phil 2:13). People never grow or go beyond their vision of God and His purpose for them. No church will ever be larger than its vision. The vision of leaders directs the future of the church.

The Holy Spirit is the creator of vision. "In the last days, God says, I will pour my Spirit on everyone. Your sons and daughters will speak what God has revealed. Your young men will see visions. Your old men will dream dreams" (Acts 2:17). We ask the Holy Spirit to plant, in our minds and hearts, the seed thoughts of a vision of our church's work. Leaders with vision have no trouble praying, because they have something to pray about. They have no trouble believing God for big blessings, because they know that God does the impossible. Leaders with vision set measurable, realistic, motivating and attainable goals as a challenge of their faith.

Vision begins with having a clear purpose and identity, and believing God has given it, and then committing yourself to fulfilling it. Pray intensely until you are convinced your vision is God's will for your congregation, and then concentrate on its fulfillment. Plan your work to accomplish your vision, and then put your faith into action.

Jonathan Fisk said, "Vision is the art of seeing things invisible." God says, "We don't look for things that can be seen but for things that can't be seen. Things that can be seen are only temporary. But things that can't be seen last forever" (2 Cor 4:18). A vision allows the church to exploit untapped possibilities.

The vision must be from God, and it must be consistently and convincingly reinforced –– and then become increasingly clear to more members.

Many opportunities should be used to share the vision through sermons, leadership retreats, church media and communications, regularly reviewing the church's progress in relation to the vision.

Things for you to do as you develop your vision and mission statement: open your mind to God: ask "What is God's will?" (Prov 28:26; 2:8); research: ask "What do I need to know before I act?" (Prov. 13:16; 18:13); seek advice: ask "Who else can help me? – Don't reinvent the wheel" (Prov. 20:18); establish priorities: ask "What is the target and what is necessary?"; evaluate the cost: ask "Is it necessary, is it worth it?"

A vision statement paints the picture of your church to show what you want God to accomplish through its leaders and members. Rick Warren states, "Let the size of your God determine the size of your goals."

A mission statement shows you the reason for your existence. It helps place boundaries around your ministry and define what you will do and what you will not do. It describes the needs you are trying to meet, and it gives a description of how you respond to those needs. It acts as the hook on which the primary objectives and goals of the church can be hung. It helps you communicate to those inside and outside of the church its purpose for being.

Leaders help create an environment conducive to understand, own and live the vision. As many people in the church as possible are to be given the opportunity to assume a meaningful role in fulfilling the vision.

Vision leads to the writing of a congregation mission statement, which displays a summary of the essential functions for church renewal. After writing and adopting a short mission statement, leaders should also write a short statement for each of the twelve quality characteristics and leading indicators of a healthy church.

Additional Material: God Says Move (pp. 165-168) will provide a few suggestions for writing a mission statement.

Reality Check

How do you rate your congregation on its "Mission Vision Statement" and "Master Mission Strategy" at this time? What are the strengths? What are the weaknesses? What new steps do you propose to take? Are national and international missions a vital part of your mission strategy?

MISSION AND VISION-DRIVEN RESOURCES

Primary Resources

1. **God Says Move** (pps. 165-168) provides a few suggestions for writing a mission statement.

2. George Barna, **Turning Vision Into Action: The Defining and Putting into Practice the Unique Ministry God Has for Your Ministry** (Regal

Books), George Barna's video and book, The **Power of Vision: How Finding God's Vision Can Transform Your Ministry**, is available from Gospel Light.

3. Kent Hunter, **Your Church Has Personality**, (Fairway Press/Church Growth Center, Corunna, Indiana). This book helps the church understand itself, identify its mission, and cast its vision.

4. **Vision Day, Capturing the Power of Vision**, by Elmer Towns (Church Growth Institute).

Minimum Level Activity

5. Write or review a congregation Master Mission Statement. Resources are **God Says Move** (pps. 165-168), **Turning Vision Into Action**, and the video, **The Power of Vision**.

Moderate Level Activity

6. Consider use of **Your Church Has Personality**, by Ken Hunter, to help your congregation cast its vision.

7. Consider using either George Barna's or Elmer Towns' resources on building vision, which are named under Primary Resources.

8. Write a Master Mission Strategy.

Leading Indicator #3/Pillar #11

BIBLICAL FINANCIAL STEWARDSHIP
(Luke 12:15; 2 Cor 8:1-2, 5, 8, 12; 9:6,10-13)

"He told the people, 'Be careful to guard yourselves from every kind of greed. Life is not about having a lot of material possessions'" (Luke 12:15).

"Brothers and sisters, we want you to know how God showed His kindness to the churches in the province of Macedonia. While they were being severely tested by suffering, their overflowing joy, along with their extreme poverty, has made them even more generous....They did more than we had expected. First, they gave themselves to the Lord and to us, since this was God's will....I'm not commanding you, but I'm testing how genuine your love is by pointing out the dedication of others....with whatever contributions you have. Since you are willing to do this, remember that people are accepted if they give what they are able to give. God doesn't ask for what they don't have" (2 Cor 8:1-2, 5, 8, 12).

"Remember this: The farmer who plants a few seeds will have a very small harvest. But the farmer who plants because he has received God's blessings will receive a harvest of God's blessings in return....God gives seed to the farmer and food to those who need to eat. God will also give you seed and multiply it. In your lives He will increase the things you do that have His approval. God will make you rich enough so that you can always be generous. Your generosity will produce thanksgiving to God because of us. What you do to serve others not only provides for the needs of God's people, but also produces more and more prayers of thanksgiving to God. You will honor God through this genuine act of service because of your commitment to spread the Good News of Christ and because of your generosity in sharing with them and everyone else. With deep affection they will pray for you because of the extreme kindness that God has shown you" (2 Cor 9:6,10-14).

Our stewardship of giving is part of our sanctification and servanthood, as we make our churches financially strong through ongoing stewardship education, and challenging members to make sacrificial investments for eternity. Rather than concentrating on budgets, we challenge members to give God the firstfruits – a generous percentage of their income set by faith as an act of God's grace. We are willing to address the issue of money and possessions in a Biblical, relevant and practical way.

Serious budget deficits, operational debts and money pressures are experienced by many congregations. When only a small percentage of members give generous, firstfruit offerings of their income, there is a major spiritual crisis which has a negative effect on the church. Instead of shaping Christian stewards by grace, members' giving has often been molded by legalistic appeals and tactics.

Traditional church stewardship practices, in one way or another, have paralyzed the funding of the Gospel mission of Christ's church. While churches have raised more money to maintain their minimum programs, they have failed to gain their real financial potential based on the full resources God has placed into the hands of His people.

Long-term and recent research reveal a reluctance of churches to deal forthrightly and Biblically with the use of money and of Christian giving [18]:

- 55% of pastors fear they will be viewed as self-serving, seeking to raise their own salaries when they preach and teach about money, while 27% of lay persons think so.

- 30% of clergy think that members consider money and possessions as unspiritual.

- Many clergy are reluctant to preach sermons on money, because people resist changes in their personal lifestyles and giving practices.

- Congregations have increased costs, having difficulty to get more money.

- Biblical giving, including use of money, is a major problem in most churches with a mission-funding crisis.

- Theological education has not adequately prepared pastors for their stewardship ministry.

Some of the biggest drags on God's mission are found in poor stewardship practices, even in successful churches. It is a major crisis which is allowed to exist without intervention. Only a small percentage of church members give generous firstfruit offerings. Most members use about 98% of their incomes for themselves while giving leftovers to the church. About 10% give 75% of the congregation's funds. Less than 20% of congregations teach/cultivate members in the use of money and giving.

Members' giving has been guided by budgets, legalistic appeals, and dealing with symptoms rather than Biblical issues. Pressure tactics, budget appeals, needs-centered programs, second and third offerings, sales, bazaars, raffles, and Octoberfests have been used too often.

Jesus did not say, "Go, buy and sell, use a budget to appeal for money, so that the church can get enough money to fund the Gospel mission of the Kingdom," but He said, "Go, make disciples... teaching...baptizing...seek the Kingdom first."

Are we ready to address the giving failures/paralysis/sickness which drains churches of spiritual vitality for the use of the full resources that God has made available for the local and worldwide ministry of the Gospel? Are we ready to use the budget only to empty the treasury rather than an appeal to fill the treasury? Do we realize that the problem is one of empty heads (lack of information and knowledge), not of empty church bank accounts?

Healthy congregations will recognize the conflicting approaches between maintenance stewardship and grace/educational stewardship:

Maintenance/Traditional/Needs	Biblical/Grace/Educational
To (Needs/Budget)	From What God Has Given (Through the church to God)
Your Share of the Budget	God's Share of Your Income
What do we do? (Doing)	Who am I? (Being)
Meetings	Ministry
Divide Scarcity and Poverty	Multiply Resources and God's Abundance
Parts of Life and Resources	Entire Life and All Resources
Money for the Church (Growing Budgets)	People for God (Growing Christians)
Leftovers	Firstfruits
Mirror/Tunnel Vision	World Vision
Dismal, Dull, Failed System	Dynamic Grace System

Every member is to view giving of money and church fund-raising activities as something spiritual, not unspiritual. Fund-raising in the Old and New Testaments has always been a significant part of spiritual ministry. David, Nehemiah, Ezra, Haggai and other Old Testament leaders raised resources for the Lord's work in response to God's call. Jesus taught much about money and giving. Paul's teachings in 1 Corinthians 16:1-3 and 2 Corinthians 8 and 9 teach basic Biblical principles of giving to the Lord and His church.

Jesus always had two kingdoms in mind, with two masters, two treasuries, two characters, two perspectives, and two values. These two realities are the natures of earth and heaven, which give us two kingdom truths and principles.

Jesus gave us a choice – a life wasted chasing wealth on earth, or a life invested in the pursuit of wealth in heaven. The key question is: Where is your treasure (Matt 6:20)? Thus, there are two faces of money – as an instrument of good or evil. The God of one is the Creator (Father) of the eternal Kingdom, while the other is the god of materialism (Satan).

Jesus' reference to the vine and branches in John 15 and the Psalmist's words in 1:3, tell us that healthy branches with green leaves and good fruit are a by-product of a good root system, healthy trunk, nourishment, sunlight and rain.

Jesus' Word in John 15:1-8 reveals what the money/giving problem is in the institutional church. A good tree (a repentant and forgiven Christian, fed and led by Law and Gospel, having victory of the new nature over the old nature) bears good fruit; a sick tree (a person living more under the Law than under grace, not practicing Biblical principles of giving, but trying to live up to expectations) will bear bad fruit. Jesus tells all about the importance of the root system (nourishment, rain, sunshine/instruction and information), vine/trunk (Jesus), branches (believers), and fruit (gifts). Jesus is interested in teaching strong Christians (healthy branches) that will bear generous fruit for the Kingdom. Jesus despises the spirit of discontent, greed, self-centeredness, self-indulgence, and covetousness.

Materialism and consumerism are the spirit of the American cultural virus which infects many Christians. Unless and until our members are strengthened spiritually, being informed of God's will in the use of money and giving, and empowered by God's Word of grace, then church steward-ship maintenance and survival will continue to appeal to need and pride.

We cannot expect more money from people whose belief system is weak with a crisis of faith. The best predictor of generous giving is strong belief and informed minds. The very heart of what it takes to be a faithful man-ager/steward is a healthy Christian fed in a healthy congregation.

What to do? Recognize that money follows relevant ministry, a clear sense of mission, and leaders who model servant giving. Forget the finan-cial crisis, and return to the Biblical model of building believers instead of raising money for the church. Begin the drastic change in your congrega-tion's and people's giving from the materialism/institutional kingdom to the Biblical Kingdom of Christ.

This means a change from raising money to raising people spiritually, from giving to needs and budgets to giving firstfruits from what God gives, from giving leftovers to giving firstfruits, from giving a few more dollars to changing giving habits, from fair shares and quotas to generous percentage offerings and tithing, from campaigns for money to educating people to give by Biblical principles, and from needs in search of givers to givers in search of needs. Pursue Biblical standards, not pragmatic ones.

The choice is clear. Will we have a Kingdom of God mentality with "supply-side stewardship," where God's Supply House is the divine source of our entire being and every action of serving and giving – or will it be the "human container kingdom model," that assumes there is a fixed and lim-ited supply to be divided, fought over and redistributed by people who are spiritually impoverished? The first is an explosive belief that what we are doing here on earth is for Arrival – living under God's grace to express our faith here on earth until that day we will arrive at God's throne, righteous by Christ's blood in the eternal Kingdom. The other is the materialistic king-dom of Survival - feverishly planning and working to make ends meet, hop-ing to have enough left over to give a little more to the church, and hoping and praying that, somehow, some day, we will survive and God will accept us on the Last Day by His mercy.

After a six-week stewardship teaching on faith, commitment, purpose, service, gratitude and sacrifice in the name of Jesus, Pastor Rick Warren and Saddleback Church in Lake Forest, California, raised $28.5 million in one weekend. Pursuing stewardship/giving for Arrival by members in your church, your preaching and teaching for reviving your members and renewing your church should contain three conditions: awareness of the holiness of God, repentance for sins and changing sinful habits, and acceptance of the free forgiveness in Christ; three primary elements of Gospel application: in Christ you are fully accepted, free from bondage to sin to do good works, and God will provide strength through the indwelling Holy Spirit, and you have strength for victory. When the full dimensions of God's gracious provision in Christ are clearly articulated, and people are living for Arrival, there will be intense living for Christ, serving and giving, having the mind of Christ to be active in His mission.

Which is your approach? The Kingdom where God is never short in supply of His provisions and always generous with His love, or the materialistic kingdom which is a failed legal system of expectations on the basis of try a little harder, maintain the church, and hope for the best? Over 80% of today's churches ought to be challenged by a better way to teach and present God's Word and will of generous firstfruits giving to enlarge local and worldwide Gospel missions.

Healthy congregations will teach all members the Biblical principles of giving through a series of sermons, Bible studies, every member contacts, and printed materials to help people understand and commit themselves to the use of their abilities, time management, personal money management, and generous firstfruit percentage giving.

Additional Material: **God Says Move** (Ch. 10), "Biblical Stewardship Theology and Practices Help Make the Church Functional," provides basic stewardship analyses, proposals and resource ideas to guide your church toward effective Biblical stewardship training and programs.

Reality Check

How do you rate your congregation on "Biblical Financial Stewardship" at this time? What are the strengths? What are the weaknesses? What new steps do you propose to take? Rating your congregation from 1 to 10 (10 is highest), is your congregation's stewardship/giving education and practice based on making the budget or on making faithful disciples? How are members educated in the principles of Christian giving and tithing by God's grace?

BIBLICAL FINANCIAL STEWARDSHIP RESOURCES

Primary Resources

1. **God Says Move** (Ch. 10), "Biblical Stewardship Theology and Practices Help Make the Church Functional," provides basic stewardship analyses, proposals and resource ideas to guide your church toward effective Biblical stewardship training and programs.

2. ***Christian Stewards-Confronted and Committed***, by Waldo J. Werning (Discipling/Stewardship Center). This book is a basic resource for congregational stewardship. All stewardship leaders should read it.

3. George Barna's video, ***How to Increase Giving in Your Church*** (Gospel Light, Ventura, CA, 1996, about 55 minutes), provides 14 money-raising principles plus other basic suggestions.

4. A number of series of stewardship sermons and Bible studies produced and used broadly, nationally and internationally, are available through the Discipling/Stewardship Center, 111 AF Oakton Avenue, Pewaukee, WI 53072. ph/fax: 262-691-7751; www.healthychurch.com. e-mail wjwern1@aol.com

Big Step Forward in Faith (Discipling/Stewardship Center), eight weeks of expository sermons, Bible studies and prayers. Topics are "Born to Serve Our Creator," "Our Civil War: The New Man's Victory Over the Old Man," "Live Worthy of Our Call to Serve God," "You Have a Story to Tell!", "The First and Big Stewardship Offering: Our Repentant Heart," "God's Rich Supply for Our Faithful Giving," "A Grace-Based, Word-Directed, Gospel-Driven, Spirit-Powered, Book of Acts Mission Church." Six responsive prayers are supplied.

New Beginnings – In Christian Living and Giving (Discipling/Stewardship Center), four-week stewardship/ spiritual growth plan for congregations, plus expository sermons and Bible studies on the following topics: "New Beginnings: Changing From Institutional to Biblical Christians," "New Beginnings: Trust and Obey Only God," "Do What God Wants You to Do," "Lord, Touch Our Eyes Again So That We May See Clearly" (a sermon on proportionate giving and tithing). Letters to members are also supplied.

I Am Ready to Live (Discipling/Stewardship Center), sermons, Bible studies, a leader's guide, and an every-member stewardship booklet for group meetings or every-member visits or mailings, giving a challenge to live purposely, not just exist, and to give firstfruits, not leftovers: 1) Having Christ as the center and setting Christian goals; 2) Real security, happiness, and success comes from trusting and obeying Christ; 3) Jesus wants us to have the abundant life; 4) Productive and successful living begins with God's goodness; 5) Faithful living involves faithful use of abilities and spiritual gifts; 6) Enlarge your life's influence by investing firstfruits for God's work.

New Steps of Faith (Discipling/Stewardship Center), six weeks of sermons and Bible studies, together with other helps, a leader's guide, stewardship booklet for group meetings or every-member visits or for mailings. Stress that faith is to be expressed through stewardship and the sanctified life. Trusting faith will lead members to: 1) grow and mature spiritually; 2) be a functioning member of Christ's body; 3) have a truly Christian lifestyle; 4) witness and confess Christ; 5) manage your financial resources and assets faithfully; 6) live by God's promises.

5. Help many members overcome their tragic mismanagement of their finances and poor money management. Crown Financial Ministries, 601 Broad St. SE, P.O. Box 100, Gainesville, GA 30501; ph. 1-800-340-5066' fax 1-770-503-9447; web address: www.crown.org., offers a twelve-week small group Bible study in which thousands of participants in church-sponsored groups have statistically documented that this study helped participants to decrease or eliminate debt, increase personal savings, develop a household budget and financial goals, increase the % given to the Lord's work (frequently a 100% increase), increase the amount of time volunteering for Christian service, increase time spent in daily Bible reading and prayer, and making a will or estate plan.

Minimum Level Activity

1. Guide leaders through a study of "Biblical Stewardship," (Ch. 10, **God Says Move**), together with the study helps at the end of the book, followed by the reading and study of **Christian Stewards-Confronted and Committed**.

2. Conduct an in-depth series of stewardship sermons and Bible studies, using the resources listed in the Primary Resources.

Moderate Level Activity

3. Review Barna's video, **How to Increase Giving in Your Church**.

4. Use the Crown Ministries Bible studies to teach money management.

5. Excellent resources for stewardship Bible studies are the following produced by Stewardship Advisors Publications, 2225 East 14 Mile Rd., Birmingham, MI 48009 (888-783-2790) by Ronald J. Chewning: "Life at It's Best, Living Wisely in an Unwise World"; "Controlling Your Money"; "Excell in the Grace of Giving"; "Living as Faithful Stewards."

6. Neibauer Press, 20 Industrial Drive, Warminster, PA 18974, Phone 800-322-6203, fax (215) 322-2465, sales@neibauer.com provides some excellent stewardship educational materials and resources. They will be happy to share a stewardship catalog with you.

Leading Indicator #4/Pillar #12

CHURCH PLANTING
(Acts 19:10; Col 1:6-8, 1 Thess 1:6-8; Acts 14:24-25)

"This continued for two years so that all the Jews and Greeks who lived in the province of Asia heard the Word of the Lord" (Acts 19:10).

"This Good News is present with you now. It is producing results and spreading all over the world as it did among you from the first day you heard it. At that time you came to know what God's kindness truly means. You learned about this Good News from Epaphras, our dear fellow servant. He is taking your place here as a trustworthy deacon for Christ and has told us about the love that the Spirit has given you" (Col 1:6-8).

"You imitated us and the Lord. In spite of a lot of suffering, you welcomed God's Word with the kind of joy that the Holy Spirit gives. This way, you became a model for all the believers in the province of Macedonia and Greece. From you the Lord's Word has spread out not only through the province of Macedonia and Greece but also to people everywhere who have heard about your faith in God. We don't need to say a thing about it" (1 Thess 1:6-8).

"After they had gone through Pisidia, they went to Pamphylia. They spoke the message in the city of Perga and went to the city of Attalia" (Acts 14:24-25).

Church planting has been at the heart of the Great Commission for the church from the time of Jesus and the Apostles to today. Jesus said, "I will build my church" (Matt. 16:18). Biblical and strategic vision requires us to focus on planting churches which will, in turn, provide the dynamic to reproduce themselves. The great need is to plant new churches, which give birth to baby churches, which result in adult churches.

Our purpose is not to organize churches with buildings and institutional traditions and forms, but rather to plant churches as Life-giving Churches and Centers for Missionary Formation, beginning with a nucleus of workers sent to nurture and minister. We are committed to reproducing ourselves, having a vision for planting or facilitating the planting of churches in our community, nation and the world, reproducing Centers for Missionary Formation.

Involvement in planting churches by a local congregation will depend, first of all, on the area demographics. Some rural areas, small towns, and possibly even some suburban areas might find it necessary to reach quite far to plant a church. However, all churches can become involved in church-planting activities by denominations or agencies, both nationally and internationally.

What can a healthy adult church, which follows the Scriptures as the only rule of faith and practice, look like? A simple and comprehensive answer, which we propose in this book, is that church planting concentrate on incorporating the 12 pillars or qualities of a healthy church. It is imperative that church planters understand this as the final goal of each church planting effort, and that this be kept in the forefront of the church planting strategy.

David J. Hesselgrave, in Planting Churches Cross-Culturally, tells that the "Pauline Cycle" of the church planting procedure found in the Book of Acts, is composed of ten elements:[20]

1. Missionaries Commissioned (13:1-4); 15:39, 40)
2. Audience Contacted (13:14-16; 14:1; 16:13-15)
3. Gospel Communicated (13:17-41; 16:31)
4. Hearers Converted (13:58; 16:14, 15)
5. Believers Congregated (13:43)
6. Faith Confirmed (14:21, 22; 15:41)
7. Leadership Consecrated (14:23)
8. Believers Commended (14:23; 16:40)
9. Relationships Continued (15:36; 18:23)
10. Sending Churches Convened (14:26-27; 15:1-4).[21]

Reality Check

How do you rate your congregation on "Church Planting" at this time? What are the strengths? What are the weaknesses? What new steps do you propose to take? Has your church ever planted another church? What are the possibilities of planting a new church in the future? What opportunities does your congregation have to plant a new congregation to reach a group of people culturally and ethnically different whom you are unable to reach and assimilate in your kind of congregation?

CHURCH PLANTING RESOURCES

Primary Resources

1. Bob Logan, **Church Planter's Kit**.
2. Bob Logan, **Churches Planting Churches**.
3. Elmer Towns, **Getting a Church Started** (Church Growth Institute).

Minimum Level Activity

1. Has your church been involved in the planting of at least one new church in recent years?
2. Have you targeted other communities for planting, or been involved in association with others to do so, or talked with your denomination stewardship leaders or an agency to plant churches overseas?

3. Study Bob Logan's **Church Planter's Kit or Churches Planting Churches**.

Special Reminder

Congregations will benefit greatly as they introduce the use of **Natural Church Development** and the **12 Pillars of a Healthy Church** by offering a series of sermons and Bible studies on the 12 pillars. A resource book, **The Healthy Church – Sermons and Bible Studies**, is available from Concordia University, 2811 NE Holman Street, Portland, OR 97211-6099 (Ph) 503-288-9371.

CHAPTER THREE

Leading a Congregation Through Transition to be a Healthier Church

In a real sense, most congregations, even healthy ones, are at some level of transition at all times. This is true because even the healthiest ones face special challenges, emergencies, a change of pastorates, an influx of new members with differing expectations, the continuing change in culture or the community, a crisis, or something else not anticipated. Breakthrough leaders will always have transition and change of their internal and external context on their minds.

Leading the church through transition will present various paradoxes while looking for the leverage points, and using the keys and steps to effective transition. Healthy churches thrive in the midst of change and new challenging opportunities. Healthy leaders are always prepared to change first. Strong leaders will recognize the resources of the congregation to effect change, and recognize that each person is at a different level of willingness to go through the transition time.

Recognize What's Unhealthy

Negative aspects have to be recognized in order to establish a climate for growth. Without a proper climate, we can do everything right and still not experience growth. The Holy Spirit provides a proper climate in response to leaders practicing and modeling Biblical principles.

Ray Ellis tells of the damaging effect of deadly diseases which keep churches unhealthy: "Unhealthy churches are filled with conflicts, spiritual carnality, leaders more interested in control than allowing the Holy Spirit to lead. The focus of toxic churches is inward. They are ingrown, lack vision, lack passion for souls, are comfortable, apathetic and satisfied to 'play church'.

"Unhealthy churches are characterized by five deadly diseases:

"1. Toleration of known sin – gossip, carnality and critical spirit. Healthy churches practice the Biblical principles found in Matthew 18:15-17.

"2. Lack of reproductive ministries. Healthy churches have a plan to equip leaders for ministry. Leaders are mobilized according to the teachings found in Ephesians 4:11-16 and 2 Timothy 2:2.

"3. Lack of desire to grow. Healthy churches have a compelling passion for kingdom growth and are committed to carrying out the Great Commission of Matthew 28:19-20.

"4. Lack of commitment to pray. Healthy churches not only talk about prayer, they pray with a deep passion for lost people who need Jesus.

"5. Overly organized for the church's size. Healthy churches have a simple organization with a focus on having time for ministry and not attending more meetings."[22]

Healthy Transition

Breakthrough pastors will meet with key leaders regularly and make sure everyone understands the importance of being positive and enthusiastic about the decision to be a healthy church. The speed of change can be determined by the level of the leaders' and members' discontent in failing to meet new ministry/mission challenges, and with the status quo. The higher the level of discontent, the faster the pace of transition and change. At the same time, healthy leaders must have patience and help impatient people to accept what they perceive to be slow progress, while keeping any dissidents from organizing opposition.

A healthy transition requires recognizing and setting proper priorities for the leaders themselves and for the church. In people-building priorities, questions will be raised about which programs are to be phased out, and what should be kept on hold, so that doing things well will be a main priority. Questions will be raised about how leaders can be better equipped, and how members can be moved to a higher level of maturity. Are we taking steps to surface more workers? Are we developing workers who think strategically and act with a ministry heart? What are our priorities for empowering and equipping leaders and members for mission?

Six Levels of Congregational Maturity

One of the vital tasks is to determine the level of the congregation's maturity. God Says Move, pp. 60-63, offers six levels of the ladder of spirituality and maturity of congregations.

The **first** level is a negative one, where the majority of the members are spiritually illiterate, unaware, or blind, even to major questions of substance and style. They have a maintenance mentality with no sense of mission, responding mainly to loyalty themes which tend to be self-centered and self-serving.

The **second** level involves some knowledge, yet there is general indifference toward the Great Commission. The "we/they" mentality is strong, involving little more than talk.

The **third** level is one where the pastor and some leaders and a few members have caught a Biblical vision, but are in the early stage. The members, as a whole, do not understand the renewal vision, while leaders are not united. There is little support for leaders.

The **fourth** level is the most difficult to achieve: Congregational change from an institutional/maintenance to Biblical/functional character, adopted by the majority. Empowerment is happening through interactive Bible studies, small groups, and some ministries are being strengthened.

The **fifth** level is the adoption of the vision of a healthy church by leaders and members alike. There is general application of the spiritual growth principles.

The **sixth** level finds the church innovative and creative in the Biblical process of empowering and mobilizing God's people for mission, developing new ministries. The congregation is a deployment center to send discipled members into the community and the world. A maximum number of members are discipled.

An important transition principle is that leaders change before the church changes, and that church renewal begins with personal renewal. Transitioning a church must also focus on the process of development of the maturity level of Christian disciples. First of all, this involves a commitment to life-long personal and group Bible study. Then it requires a commitment to ministry.

The maturity level transition of individual disciples may begin with tasks, like cleaning the church, serving food, working the nursery, etc. The next step leads to exposing one's faith to the more threatening activity of witnessing, involvement in mission projects, etc. The next level is caring for those within the church, reaching out in love. This is followed by caring for those outside, one's friends and family, by building new relationships, and visiting newcomers. The final steps are extending contacts through evangelism and discipling of others, ending with a spiritual explosion of selfless discipling of others and taking on challenging leadership positions. God Says Move, pp. 200-202, proposes what church members and converts should expect from a healthy church.

True vitalization of the church to be healthy begins with a true concept of God, accepting the full revelation of the person and work of Jesus Christ, a consciousness of the presence and power of the Holy Spirit, and the formation of the church as the body of Christ, with its Biblical marks of the Word and Sacrament as the foundation for ministry.

There are not only levels of maturity, but different models which characterize congregations. In order to stimulate thought and discussion, the following models are presented in order to help you identify the present model of your church.

Four Different Models

Although there are more than four models, we selected the following as generalization and tendencies, with the knowledge that very few congregations will have all the attributes of any one specific model. However, the tendencies are clear, and usually they can be observed quite easily. We will first outline the tendencies of each model and then provide a commentary on them:

MODEL 1
(WORSHIP AND "COME" STRUCTURE–MAINTENANCE)
Word and Sacrament (worship centered)

- Hardened forms of liturgy and worship
- Fellowship (more or less)
- Clergy-centered, managerial style
- Program approach for budget, evangelism, and stewardship (maintenance)
- Low Bible class attendance
- "Fill the pew and fill the plate" attitude
- Symptoms of "dead orthodoxy" – tendency toward head knowledge and little on spiritual maturity
- Sound justification – weak sanctification (over-interpreting and under-applying texts)
- Mistake churchgoing for Christianity (gathered church and "Come" at the expense of scattered church and "Go")
- Majoring in minors (programs)
- Patchwork structure and activities (segmented)
- "Tell" is communication approach – inadequate discussion tending toward legalism
- Theologizing and procedures more important than people
- "Get it right" often at the expense of "get it out"

This is a common model in confessional churches, with differences in various denominations.

A basic problem here is that what is honored in principle is often ignored or violated in practice. Worship and liturgy are in a larger or smaller degree the "all in all." There are some evidences of clergy-centered attitudes which may indicate, "I do my job; God takes care of the rest," while generally ignoring the priesthood of all believers. Churchgoing is mistaken for Christianity. In practice, there is much majoring in minors, dealing with symptoms; also an over-dependence on hierarchical authority and form.

There is little understanding of poor communicant through language and liturgies of another country and another age. Styles and forms of previous centuries and cultures are often embraced with fierce combat.

The shelter of their doctrinal systems has failed to encounter Scripture -

to such an extent that they have domesticated their knowledge of God to accommodate ecclesiastical systems. Such rote application of theology fails to relate Scripture to current needs and conditions, but is content to pass on a doctrinal inheritance tailored to events and situations in another century. What has resulted is a protective enculturation of another century's theology and practice, freezing and isolating a mind-set which does not communicate the Word effectively to reach people in our own time and culture.

MODEL 2
("GO" STRUCTURE, ACTIVISTIC–MAINTENANCE)

- Word and Sacrament (worship) –- less regard for liturgy
- Fellowship (fairly strong)
- Laity-centered (some lack of clarity about pastoral office), managerial style
- Program approach for budget, evangelism, and stewardship (maintenance) – overly activistic
- Inadequate Bible class strengths (nurturing)
- Strong sanctification – spotty justification (over-applying and under-interpreting of texts)
- Strong emphasis on scattered church - "Go!"
- Machinery and programs outshine Biblical ministry
- Talents and spiritual gifts emphasis
- Patchwork structure and activities (segmented)
- "Tell" is communication approach – often with good discussion
- "Get it out" sometimes at the expense of "get it right"

Model 2 is an activistic reaction against the sometimes doctrinaire and hardened forms and functions of Model 1. It is an over-reaction, stemming from the feeling that the laity can make things right where it is claimed the clergy have failed. This model remains centered on maintenance and programs, with human goals tied to divine imperatives, highly organized through managerial dynamics.

MODEL 3
(PIETISTIC-EXPERIENTIAL)

- Worship (subjective)
- Fellowship (emotional)
- Pietistic – religious experience and feelings
- Evangelistic fervor
- Strong love and care
- Relationships without roots
- Roller-coaster faith – starving for solid doctrine
- Methods / task-oriented

This model pushes worship and practice toward an experiential framework, subjectivizing the Christian faith.

This is basically an emotional, subjective fellowship, often based more on religious experiences and feelings than on the revealed Word of God. It is an extremely activistic spiritual model, the church members showing much love and care for each other; it is more relational than deeply doctrinal. The life of such a fellowship is very affective, with the people experiencing the ups and downs of a roller-coaster Christianity. Its emphasis on experience and sharing leaves members with little basis on which to evaluate their "religious experiences," often leading to unbalanced or false doctrine.

MODEL 4
(BALANCED "COME" AND "GO" STRUCTURE: BIBLICAL EDUCATION-MISSION MODEL)

- Word and Sacrament with liturgy and worship form in Biblical perspective
- Balanced Worship-Bible study (nurture)
- Pastor and priesthood clearly in Biblical perspective regarding functions
- Discipling/equipping/mentoring – education process
- Edifying and fellowship – including "house-to-house" in Biblical fashion
- Biblical application of spiritual gifts
- Body action (body of Christ) – support system for loving and caring
- Grace approach to stewardship, evangelism, and world (teach)
- Biblical justification and biblical sanctification (full interpretation and full application of texts)
- Balanced and sound activities and structures of gathered-scattered church, "Come and go!" flexible, integrated, unified
- "Teach," not "tell," is communication approach
- "Get it right" and "get it out"

This authentic New Testament model integrates biblical theology with church practice with no compartmentalizing or segmentation of the basic tasks of the church. There is a healthy balance of Bible teaching, worship, fellowship, relationships, evangelism, caring, sharing, and stewardship. There is sound doctrine and content in preaching and practice. There is nurture through discipling, mentoring, teaching, edifying, and making spiritually mature members, and showing the fruit and gifts of the Spirit. There are evangelism and missions to reach non-Christians (Acts 1:8). There are effective methods and efficient physical resources, with good spiritual administration. Proclamation, Word and Sacraments, are ordered in the biblical fashion.

Correct emphasis is placed on indoctrination in basic Christian doctrines and for Christian living. The New Testament follows a pattern in which messages providing instruction in the truths of salvation are followed by portions in which the life consequences are spelled out. The epistles often begin with teaching about the work of Christ and conclude with directions on how to live as Christians by God's grace and power. The proclamation of the Good News is followed by practical teaching about living and the realities of the faith.

Search for Biblical Answers

Doctrinal and spiritual renewal in churches is essential to church health. Doctrinal renewal is a necessity for those caught in the web of theological and interpretative aberrations which infect mainline churches. At the same time, smaller evangelical churches have sometimes settled for traditional doctrinal formulations without adequately researching the Scriptures to test whether they have fully embraced God's grace, Law and Gospel, in a Word-Sacrament ministry.

Now is the time to search for answers as never before: What are we here for? Why does the church exist? How can a sick church be built up again?

There is a need for a better understanding of the integrity of the church's witness in the whole world. As the Creator has established the natural order so that man has dominion over all the earth with God as Sovereign, so through regeneration and ordination He has called lay people and pastors to work in His kingdom to help build His church through Spirit-guided Christians. God's people must once again recall who they are and to whom they belong, and renew their covenant relationship with God.

Many congregations do not seem to know how to untangle the web of confused or wrong priorities. They assume that, since they are chartered as a Christian group, they will naturally keep their true mission in perspective. "The tyranny of the urgent" causes them to major in minors, to do patchwork, and to use most of their energies on maintenance of the organization rather than on creative ministry and mission outreach.

God's grace will break our crutches and expose our lack of faith, and then lead us on the road of mature faith. His Word stands in judgment on the idolatries, false values, and bad practices we have incorporated into the institutional church. The Gospel can penetrate our encultured minds and renew them. With the crumbling of some of the tarnished signposts and fences of church practices built in the past, there will emerge a vigorous church purified of its slaveries. No longer will we be parroting the latest institutional and programmatic passwords that have sent wrong signals to people.

Ten Action Steps for Transition

Christian Schwarz presents a ten-step plan for introducing the four building blocks of "Quality Characteristics," "Minimum Factor," "Biotic (Natural) Principles," and a "New Paradigm," which answer the four basic questions of what, when, how, and why.[23] Schwarz shows how to use the quality characteristics and the ten steps to design a customized "program" for your own church, not something "off-the-rack" but "tailor-made" by your leadership.

The ten steps are intentionally phrased in such a way that they can be applied to every conceivable church situation: The congregation where leaders encounter resistance; a church which constantly desires to grow but faces many problems; a dynamic, growing church looking for ways to strategize for church development and health; a newly-planted church that has just passed the initial founding phase and is seeking help for "getting their act together." In encouraging us to work out our own strategy, Schwarz says that "God needs no handbook – we do." The ten action steps are:

Step 1: Build spiritual momentum
Step 2: Determine your minimum factors
Step 3: Set qualitative goals
Step 4: Identify obstacles
Step 5: Apply biotic (natural) principles
Step 6: Exercise your strengths
Step 7: Utilize biotic (natural) tools
Step 8: Monitor effectiveness
Step 9: Address your new minimum factors
Step 10: Multiply your church

The growth of the church by the power of the Holy Spirit means putting those principles to work in our churches as much as possible, even when they go against our tradition, seem unusual, or seem like too much work.

Schwarz maintains that we are acting on our own strengths, not by the Holy Spirit, "any time we disregard the fundamental church growth principles that we learned from Scripture and which are validated by experience; any time we ignore the growth automatisms with which God Himself builds His church; and any time we try - whether through ignorance or through spiritual arrogance – to use ineffective and resource-devouring methods."[24]

Reality Check

1. Determine at which one of the six levels of maturity your congregation is. How can you reach the next level?

2. Which of the four models most closely describes your congregation?

3. Which of the ten action steps has your congregation taken?

CHAPTER FOUR

Plan Your Master Strategy for a Healthy Church

The proposals and principles in the books, **Natural Church Development, God Says Move**, and **12 Pillars of a Healthy Church**, are built upon biblical and theological foundations. They consider the biblical dynamics by which the church grows strong. They apply spiritual realities of growth, establish priorities, and set goals on the basis of possibilities for qualitative growth by the Spirit of God in each unique environment and situation. Now is the time for you to formulate sound, exciting, and attainable plans of action, which grow out of the Word and will of God.

God's Word sets the pace and gives us principles to follow. The qualitative dimension of church health and growth is found in the Book of Acts, referring to faithfulness, reverence, love, sharing, and courage. We read about the spiritual power of believers, by which evangelism broke out of the limitations of human factors. Human capacities were directed and empowered by the Holy Spirit, who calls and equips His people to serve Him.

Are we geared to put old ways in the past and to function as a healthy church? What steps should we be taking now?

Max Lucado seems to have given a wise answer to those questions in a Bible study on "Finding Peace," with the topic, "Don't Just Do Something – Stand There!" Lucado shows that God's solution to conflict is not activism, but meditation and listening to God. Before we decide on our strategy, let us take a day off for meditation. The big challenge is for each of us to practice that faith and to make a personal confession of our beliefs. This can be done glibly or we can prepare for it by "not just doing something, but standing there!" As we stand there or sit for study, meditation and prayer, our focus needs to be on our character, integrity, honesty, and on our faith and courage to make godly choices.

Gaining a Healthy Spiritual Immune System

Is our church's spiritual immune system healthy and active? The physical body must have a healthy immune system in order to avoid weaknesses which allow infections and diseases to invade the body. The same is true of the body of Christ, the Church of the Lord Jesus Christ, the Christian congregation, and the individual Christian.

A Guide to a Great Adventure — Breaking Through to a New System

We will go no farther than our faith, character, integrity and honesty will allow. As we outline our "healing and health" spiritual road map, barriers must be identified and removed. If we are to break through to the next stage – a **new** system – the divine system, a grace system, a balanced Law-Gospel system – a system with the body of Christ as its center and core. Out of this system flows the organic and natural expression and application of the biblical doctrine of the church. All barriers of mechanistic, institutional, artificial, traditional, and programatic ways are deleted. This does not mean that we have no institution, no tradition or no programs, but it means that there are only forms which are biblical, not technocratic.

This is more than a powerful image. It is an organic transformation of church systems. It is more than a power paradigm, refining all of the best church activities of the last four centuries. It is instilling a brand new system which is actually 2000 years old ñ the New Testament model in which biblical truths are put into practice organically. The next paragraphs will be an attempt to describe how we must understand "system change." The Gospel mission for quality ministry, not growth, is the primary purpose. The organic and body of Christ nature of Christianity is the source from which flows the purpose and functions of what it means to be a Christian and to be the church. God's grace in Christ is the dynamic of this flow.

In a climate of expectation, we truly believe that we can get from here to there. As we ask God to deliver us from a traditional wilderness, we will map and travel the spiritual road to health. It may begin with a street or boulevard, leading to a freeway or autobahn of spiritual reality. It does make a big difference that we know the biblical model, from which we produce the highway to church health.

We focus basically on the need to change the life systems of the church so that existence in the church will match the grace system, not trying to restructure the institutional church or updating traditions or programs, or refining the structure, or rejuvenating boards or committees, or revitalizing strategies.

This is a ministry of transformation, not a ministry of new programs. It is a time to discern between God's call and an addiction to past ideals and traditions and misplaced loyalties. Programatic changes will not eventually lead to change in the system. Duties, positions and offices must be filled through the identification of spiritual gifts. The present system cannot be changed by the use of layers of new and innovative procedural, mechanistic or structural changes, which hold us to mediocrity.

Can we agree that there will not be healthy Christians unless there are healthy churches? That there will be no healthy churches unless there are healthy leaders? That's why we focus on a holistic approach in which God transforms the church, not where we restructure it.

The grace system will shape everything the church does. This gives life to creative ideas, whereas traditional ways are death to visionary and resourceful ideals. The grace system is an "energy field" based on the explosive Word, instead of spinning down the ecclesiastical "information and program highway." The traditional ways of the past four centuries are inadequate and insufficient because they only go back to a short time of church experience instead of the First Century and the basic Text we should be using. It is time to kick the habits of the addicted church ñ addicted to programs, committees and institutions ñ and to start birthing the biblical system of grace for a healthy church.

Biblical Power Paradigms for Our System Towards Health

The power paradigm for church health grows out of concepts displayed in Christian Schwarz' book, **Natural Church Development** (ChurchSmart Resources 3830 Ohio Ave., St. Charles, IL 60174), which gives the eight quality characteristics of a healthy church and proposes the bipolar approach that balances the static and dynamic factors of the Christian church and life. The other source from which we draw our conceptual thoughts is Christian Schwarz' **Paradigm Shift in the Church — How Natural Church Development Can Transform Theological Thinking** (ChurchSmart Resources), which challenges us to adopt the organic, body of Christ natural New Testament system instead of the historic, institutional system which we have inherited.

These pages provide a brief review, not a total description, of Schwarz's **Natural Church Development**. Although we may not agree with all the theological views in **Paradigm Shift**, its bipolar concept is an important contribution to the theological discussion on the nature of the church. Mine is a brief summary of the books both by Christian Schwarz and Rick Warren. These books should be read in the original texts.

Schwarz shows the organic nature of the church to be the simplicity and spirituality of the body of Christ, not needing the bureaucracy or technology of a modern corporation. He links spiritual growth with the Christian call and the Gospel mission. He tells that healthy churches, unlike declining church systems, require a ministry map that relies on spiritual formation, common agreement about values, beliefs, vision and mission, and risk-taking.

Schwarz tells of declining church systems which are preoccupied with belonging and institutional membership. He suggests a system change which actually is a change of the church infrastructure. It is the difference between machine/technocratic management and spiritual leadership. The key is to know what God does and what we are to do. If we do it the mechanistic way, barriers are created that do not allow God's power to work. If we ask him to do everything, then the fields will remain unplanted and unharvested. God provides all church growth. We do what we can, and God does what we can't.

Schwarz defines the six organic principles, and describes the new paradigm and ten action steps in **Natural Church Development**. He tells that technocratic logic and thinking is like believing that more traffic signs lead to greater safety, and that stronger antibiotics give better health, majoring in protection rather than teaching drivers better habits and building better immune systems.

Schwarz relates the following natural principles to church spiritual development: Interdependence, Reproduction through multiplication (giving birth to new congregations), Energy transformation (using crises creatively), Multi-usage (discipling and mentoring), Symbiosis (variety of spiritual gifts, each working according to their own gifts), and Functionality (quality and quantity of fruits ñ Mat. 7:16-17).

Schwarz introduces the theological paradigm of looking at the church in an organic or natural way as in John 15. He outlines the bipolarity in the Bible, in which every force has a counter force. The static, technical pole is a concept like that in architecture, biblically referring to stones of the temple built into God's building ñ and Christian doctrine about what a church and a Christian are. The dynamic, organic pole is the living body of Christ growing in God's field. Thus static and dynamic poles, organism and organization, are interrelated and interacting, and always in balance.

When Schwarz refers to the left and the right in his books, **Natural Church Development** and **Paradigm Shift in the Church**, he ties them to theological thinking and the application of doctrine to church life. Our reference here is to theological conceptions which become church practices. Telling that we need a bipolar balance of the static and dynamic goals, Schwarz produces the paradigm and gives us the glasses to see how the static pole can stop at doctrine which is not related to practice, and becomes too technocratic while ignoring deep spiritual issues of character and integrity. The dynamic pole of sanctification, and church practice, can stimulate great spirituality while ignoring true doctrine. Biblical glasses will help us to see the bipolar position, avoiding the dangers to the right and to the left.

Schwarz shows the necessity of a bipolar or balanced approach of Law-Gospel and of the static and dynamic factors necessary to be a healthy church. The opposite poles or standards of Law and Gospel, and static and dynamic factors in their contrast give a balance of application of divine Truths. Two unlike spiritual parts ñ static and dynamic – combine by God's grace to equalize or counterbalance as parallels to make Christians and churches healthy and productive.

A church has a healthy immune system when it is grace-based, Word-grounded, Spirit-powered and mission-directed with helpful interrelationships fed by the Gospel for justification and sanctification. This is displayed in justifying faith and in sanctifying faith ñ being certain of salvation and being strong by grace as a servant of Christ.

The static, technocratic pole is the institutional side, which can result in widely diverse forms that easily become a security mentality which believes that right doctrine will result automatically in achieving what God desires. It is a simplistic concept of cause and effect – a technocratic paradigm which comes close to magical thinking about desired results. It looks at some forms that should guarantee church health. Some of those on the right see "doctrinal correctness and purity" as a guarantee for church health. The essentials of the static pole are biblical doctrine (justification and sanctification as core beliefs), the sacraments, pastoral and lay ministry, etc.

The problem is when we believe that if we have correct doctrine, we automatically have the Holy Spirit and correct practice. Here the difficulty is the failure to be content with the certainty of faith, but seek also the security to be able to reassure ourselves with guarantees, which lead to funtamentalism, clericalism, dogmatism, and traditionalism.

These are the felt needs of the right and the static pole. The temptation is to want church organization to guarantee permanent truth, rather than the church functioning as God's organism to stimulate its organic side ñ the spiritual life of the people. This leads to a longing for a manageable authority which becomes legalistic. The struggle is to preserve not only doctrine, but insist on traditional forms in which legal precepts and the institution take the place that should be occupied only by Jesus.

"Dead orthodoxy" ñ a spiritual paralysis or blindness ñ adopts sacred linguistic forms and thought and behavior patterns which represent a formalistic externalizing of the faith to the extent that sometimes it is rationalistic. It is as though if we believe a certain doctrinal formula or affirm the historical inerrancy of the Bible, the result will be healthy Christians and healthy churches. There is a tendency toward a rational standard of knowledge alone rather than discovering and using spiritual gifts, a rejection of religious experience, a shift from faith as personal to the abstract and intellectual, and strict hierarchical leadership and discipline in order to protect from doctrinal deviation. There is no proper integration of theology into practice. Power seems to lie in the doctrinal formulas themselves, not in the Holy Spirit and the faith of the believer.

The dynamic pole is made up of the concepts of faith, fellowship and service. The temptation is to make religious experience the standard by which every other thing is judged, fed by a desire for unconditional freedom and spontaneity. The dangers of the left are found in the life of the dynamic pole where they may not always adhere to orthodox doctrine or to evangelical boundaries, and may consider institutional elements second-rate or unnecessary. The attitude is such that trust is only given to the free flowing Spirit of God, with little concern for standards or boundaries. There is a desire to establish the autonomy of the individual as free from church ordinance, institutional identities, or sometimes even basic spiritual truths. Unlike the right with rationality, the left can have such an overestimation of religious feelings that it becomes irrational. There is a belief that freedom of the Spirit prevents commitment to any sort of external forms, and appears to be a protest against institutionalism. This spiritualism separates faith from doctrine and becomes relativism, and sometimes enthusiasm.

Balance of the Static and Dynamic Poles

Do we understand that Christians who think and act in different poles — the static and the dynamic ñ and lean to the one more than the other are not pursuing balanced theology and, in effect, are talking different languages? Even where they use the same words, they may mean something completely different. The bipolar approach is essential for a proper theological understanding of church health. Both poles are necessary for church health, and both are implied in the New Testament concept of church (ekklesia) ñ organism and organization, the work of the Holy Spirit and human activity.

All of us need to pursue the bipolar model of natural church development. All of us certainly have tendencies in one direction or another. As Schwarz indicates, this is not a black-and-white yardstick, but an attempt to show the dangers to the right and the left, towards institutionalism or spiritualism. He says that the more the bipolar paradigm of natural church development is integrated into the life of the church, the higher is its level of immunity to disease, and the better it will be able to resist infections.

The bipolar position of the static and dynamic factors is the direction which shows where the boundaries are. Institutionalism says that only the static boundary counts, and spiritualism says that only the dynamic movement counts. Every Christian and every church needs to adopt the system in which right doctrine plus right behavior exists. Thus we affirm the boundaries while at the same time accept the bipolar approach. There is to be no compromise or synthesis between the two poles, but a balance.

The Struggle Between the Static and Dynamic, the Right and the Left, Institutionalism and Spiritualism

When we understand and adopt the factors of both the static and dynamic poles and keep them in balance, this will lead towards church health. This means that we avoid a merely pragmatic mindset which replaces the principle-oriented approach. We certainly ask, "What is the outcome of all of our activities?" Pragmatists quickly focus on the question, "What is the most effective way of growing the church?" (short-term thinking), determined by their own research and study, having a tendency towards human opinions on what is important for the Kingdom of God. Thus they tend to overlook the fact "God's ways are higher than our ways."

Opportunistic thinking usually centers on quantitative goals and popular methods, while the biblical approach of natural church development is qualitative and principle-oriented. The fruit is good because the tree is good (Mat. 7:17). Thus we avoid adjusting our goals to questionable current trends and using manipulative marketing methods, and sometimes cooperating with church political systems.

Schwarz indicates how Jesus frequently used parables from nature and agriculture to illustrate the nature of the Kingdom of God; "See the lilies of the field, how they grow" (Mat. 6:28). Jesus talked about the growth of the mustard seed, the tree and its fruit, the laws of sowing and reaping, the seed that grows by itself. The twelve quality characteristics and leading indicators reveal the organic potential of spiritual growth in Christ's kingdom by the Holy Spirit.

Four Key Spiritual Factors for Church Growth

Karl Koch (THE MENTOR GROUP, of Columbus, Ohio) presents the key factors in turning a congregation from maintenance to mission, which are requirements for a healthy church or for churches to grow. It is interesting to note that at least one Lutheran observer of church growth, Karl Koch, has recognized how its principles and materials fit Luther's explanation of the Third Article. He writes:

"There are four key factors to church growth that fit quite well into an outline of Luther's explanation of the Third Article.

"Introduction: ëI believe that I cannot...' Our attempts to build the Church will be as successful as our attempts to come to saving faith apart from the work of the Holy Spirit. It's, after all, God's Church not ours.

"**Key Factor #1:** "**The Holy Spirit has called me...and...the whole Christian Church on earth.**' *The role of the creative Spirit of God.* **Natural Church Development**, by C. Schwarz, is solidly anchored on the fact that my faith, and that of all believers, is the work of God the Holy Spirit. Its basic assumption is that healthy churches will grow because it is in their God-created nature to do so.

"**Key Factor #2:** "**...by the Gospel,...**' *How the Spirit of God works.* **The Twelve Pillars**, by Waldo Werning, stresses the essential working of the Spirit. An emphasis on Law and Gospel and their proper application is central to the spiritual strength and growth of the Church. This Gospel-orientation must also be introduced throughout the theology and practice of the growing church.

"**Key Factor #3:** "**Enlightens, sanctifies, and keeps me...and the whole Christian Church on earth...with his gifts.**' *When every part of the Body of Christ functions.* As St. Paul outlines it, the gifts to the Church begin with those who have received special messages and insights from God and then devolve to all believers for their equipping that they might be the final gifts of God to one another. This, I believe, is the special burden of Rick Warren (see **The Purpose Driven Church**) and Waldo Werning in their ministries and writings.

"Key Factor #4: "...in which Christian Church He daily and richly forgives all sins to me and all believers.' *Spiritually healthy leaders and members build healthy churches.* Healthy leaders and members understand that forgiveness is one of the core values of their faith, and of their relationships within the congregation. The concepts and materials of Peter Steinke deal with this subject directly. They have proven to be of real value in congregations that have suffered stress and conflict, from which they need to recover before they can grow."

It is the nature of the church as the creation of the Holy Spirit to grow qualitatively, and it is therefore natural for leaders to desire the church to be healthy. This requires a balanced proclamation of Law and Gospel, and of justification and sanctification, and of what Christian Schwarz calls the static and dynamic factors of the church.

It is the nature of the church as the creation of the Holy Spirit to grow qualitatively, and it is therefore natural for leaders to desire the church to be healthy. This requires a balanced proclamation of Law and Gospel, and of justification and sanctification, and of what Christian Schwarz calls the static and dynamic factors of the church.

That brings us to Rick Warren's, "THE PURPOSE-DRIVEN CHURCH, Growth Without Compromising Your Message & Mission." (Grand Rapids: Zondervan, 1995) Emphasizing that the church is a living spiritual organism, Warren states, "The wrong question: What will make our church grow? The right question: What is *keeping* our church from growing?" He states, "The task of church leadership is to discover and remove growth-restricting diseases and barriers so that natural, normal growth can occur," by the Holy Spirit. Warren believes the key issue for churches in the 21st Century is "church *health* not church *growth*," saying that "healthy churches don't need gimmicks to grow." [25]

Warren informs us that every methodology needs a theology, for every theology has a context and requires a method to reach people. He says that "Vision is not as much the ability to see the future as being alert to opportunities within your current circumstances." [26] Our vision grows out of the Word and leads us into our mission for Christ. Warren raises such relevant questions as, "How much of what churches do is really biblical? How much of what we do is just cultural? What are the barriers to growth?" [27] Important is his statement, "A church's health is measured by its *sending* capacity, not its *seating* capacity." [28]

Showing the partnership between God and man, Warren writes, "We cannot do it *without God*, but He has decided not to do it *without us*! Paul illustrated this partnership between God and man when he said, ëI planted the seed, Apollos watered it, but God made it grow...We are God's fellow workers. (1 Cor. 3: 6,9)"[29] He then makes reference to a number of New Testament passages which talk about building God's Kingdom, growing Christ's body, harvesting God's fields, etc. In this ministry, he reminds us, "Never confuse the methods with the message. The message must never change, but the methods must change with each new generation." [30]

As we seek to come to agreement on the purpose and meaning for the church in the LCMS, in the last chapter of this book, Warren gives us this reminder, "A church without a purpose and mission eventually becomes a museum piece of yesterday's tradition…A clear purpose not only defines what we *do*, it defines what we *don't do*." [31] In defining the purpose of the church, he urges us to look at Christ's ministry and the examples of the New Testament churches. Possibly his most quotable statement is "What a Church Family Gives": "God's *purpose* to live for (missions); God's people to live with (membership); God's *principles* to live by (maturity); God's *profession* to live out (ministry); God's *power* to live on (magnified). [32]

CHAPTER FIVE

Empowering and Mobilizing are the Keys that Unlock the Door to a Healthy Church

There is always the tendency to mobilize faster than we empower people for mission. The need for mobilizing is very obvious, while there is much less pressure on the act of empowering. Some very strong and healthy congregations have sometimes realized that they had not empowered a sufficient number of leaders and members to pursue their mobilization plans.

Empowering means training for the fulfillment of the Great Commission, among all age groups, recognizing that every believer has unique potential. It requires a commitment to a philosophy of ministry that revolves around Great Commission priorities, believing that Jesus not only gave the message and the mandate, but also modeled the method of ministry through empowering His disciples.

Christ spent time building relationships with everyone, creating a relational environment for growth. He invested considerable time in equipping a few, while not ignoring others. Then He moved on to aggressive outreach through lifestyle evangelism, while equipping His disciples in skills of cultivation, sowing and reaping. He selected leaders to multiply ministry through them.

Two words – **empower and mobilize** – provide the key principle for building a healthy church. Rick Warren shows a balance in empowering and mobilizing through his "ballfield" illustration with a commitment to empowering membership (Knowing Christ) as first base, empowering maturity (Growing in Christ through Bible studies) as second base, mobilizing ministry (Serving Christ) as third base, and mobilizing for missions (Sharing Christ) as home base.

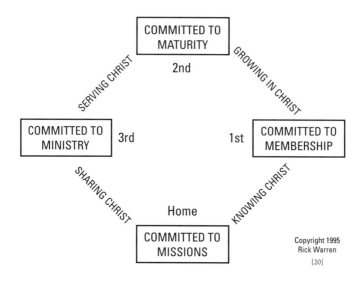

Base One involves empowering membership so that people know Christ. Some churches have such small requirements for church membership that it seems that some people are carried there or go on crutches. Far too many are listed as members who have no or a small commitment to the church. Some move to the bleachers and come down only for Christmas and Easter. Others lounge around first base with no desire to go to second, third or home base. Membership should mean a committed life to Christ through active worship and Bible study, and ministry and mission ñ after having concluded a basic study of Christian doctrine and faith.

Base Two involves empowering members for maturity. The focus is on developing character of more than mere knowledge and external actions and behavior. Intensive training and mentoring relationships are to be established.

Base Three involves mobilizing for ministry — a commitment to service and to be a servant. Members are to discover and use their spiritual gifts (Eph. 4:7).

Home Base involves mobilizing for missions — sharing Christ by witnessing or evangelism.

As the goals and resources of this ballfield graph are developed for the empowering and mobilizing of God's people for mission, we can find insights into how God transforms a church. Building on the foundation of the *12 Pillars of a Healthy Church* and Christian Schwarz' *Natural Church Development*, Rick Warren's grid can be developed into a full-fledged "Christian Life Development Process" of moving from membership to missions for vision-casting to change from traditionalistic, ritualistic, mechanistic, institutionalistic, and programistic church models. This process displays Biblical principles which involve grace and the body of Christ as the skeleton. This presumes a recognition of the 12 quality characteristics and leading indicators of a healthy church, strengthening many minimum factors so that each makes a positive contribution to church health.

Base One – Committed to Membership (Embrace/Enfold /Encircle/Incorporate Members Who Know and Confess Christ)

> **Knowing Christ**
> **1.**
> **EMPOWERING MEMBERSHIP**

Goals:
Knowing
Confessing
Living
Belonging

Resources:
1. Catechism (101)
2. Spiritual Travel Guide (102)
3. Experiencing God (103)
4. Spiritual fitness Exercise (104)
5. GRASP Spiritual Gifts (105)

Leaders:
Pastors, Elders, Education Board

The first and big challenge is to help people to reach first base. Most churches allow many members to live with minimal standards of behavior patterns rather than a faith life of passionate spirituality. Mostly, there is little semblance of spirituality outlined in the Book of Acts and Paul's epistles.

First Base commitment means that members receive Bible-based and life-centered instruction, establishing them in the Christian faith, and helping them to establish meaningful relationships with love and care. People are not merely to see themselves as church members, but as members of the body of Christ. Each is to be accountable to each other in the Body. Members are to be monitored so that they reach second, third and home bases. They should recognize that reaching first base is the first step to a lifelong relationship with Christ and with fellow Christians.

The healthy congregation provides functions, activities and structures that foster building relationships in the church's circle of love and care. The healthy church does more than maintaining membership but also addresses the needs of people in their daily challenges by way of nurturing and supporting those who are new to the Christian faith. The congregation and its leaders bear responsibility for providing the rich soil in which individuals grow and are nourished in their lives.

Membership standards include four basic disciplines of the Christian faith: corporate worship, study of the Scriptures, prayer, and service/ministry in daily life. This journey/passage includes separation from sinful habits of the past, incorporation/assimilation in the congregation, Bible study that moves the member from first base to second base to third base. All center on spiritual formation as a result of regular biblical information. The target is to be the mind, emotions, and will, engaging people in their full person and personality.

The healthy congregation provides structures and activities that foster building relationships in the congregation's circle of care. This is a pattern of church life that focuses not on self, but on the care and growth of others. The healthy congregation performs more than maintaining membership but also addresses the questions and needs of people in their daily temptations and challenges. Members can then live in an environment where the pastor, leaders, and all members minister to each other as they are organized for faithful care of the membership.

The healthy congregation offers apprenticeship or sponsors for all new members in the Christian faith. This is not just a program whereby the church adds to its list of members, but a way of welcoming, nurturing and supporting those who are new to the Christian faith. They are to be encouraged to encounter Christ's dying and rising – the struggle between God and the powers of darkness which takes on life and breath in the faithful participation and practice of the Christian life. The congregation as a whole bears responsibility for providing the rich soil in which individuals can grow and be nourished in their new life.

Establishing a Standard of Ten Biblical Expectations for Church Membership

Currently, church membership standards and expectations are not clear or uniform on the part of pastors and leaders on one side and of members on the other side. The reality of the situation shows that biblical expectations and actual performances are miles apart. Little contact is made in many congregations to members who attend worship and commune infrequently. In some congregations over one-third of the members give little or no offerings while 70 percent give token offerings.

Saying the right words and doing the right things will give members a passing membership grade in most churches. A failure to determine and expect a true biblical standard of spirituality for membership doesn't make sense – and in some cases is a scandal to the Gospel. Can we agree that this low level of membership expectations is one of the chief and direct reasons for poor church health? Obviously, it is time to set a biblical standard now.

My proposal for a **Standard of Ten Biblical Expectations for Church Membership**, subject to further revision, is:

1. Know God's flow of grace (and Gospel power) for salvation (justification) and living for Christ (sanctification). Be certain of salvation by grace through faith in Jesus Christ (Eph. 2:8-10) and the Holy Spirit's strength to do good works. By the Law and Gospel, live daily in repentance and forgiveness in Christ.

2. Change spiritually from inside out, beginning with the heart/character to beliefs/mind to attitude/values to behavior/actions to habits/lifestyle. Connect our lifestyle to our beliefs, for all beliefs are about practice.

3. Through lifelong Bible study and use of the sacraments, Christians move from knowledge (information) to spiritual formation (understanding, attitude, action).

4. Know the New Man's victory over the Old Man (new self over old self). Feed the new self and starve the old self.

5. God calls us to a sanctified and holy life – Rom. 12:2; 1 Tim. 6:1; 2 Cor. 4:1-8; 1 Cor. 10:31; John 15:16; Eph. 4:12-16.

6. Understand and use spiritual gifts – 1 Cor. 12:1, Eph. 4:7.

7. Be an active part of the body of Christ – Rom. 12:5,10,16; 15:7,14; Col. 3:13, 16.

8. Have fervent prayer – Matt. 7:7; Luke 18:1' Eph. 6:16, 1Thes 5:17.

9. Have passionate spirituality. Deepen spirituality by God's grace, avoiding sinful habits and entanglements – Eph. 5:15-16; Col. 3:4ff.

10. Put God first – Matt. 6:33.

The empowering goal for membership is to experience an active life in Jesus – knowing Christ, confessing Christ, living in Christ, and belonging to the body of Christ. Alan E. Klatt, Lutheran pastor in Brookfield, Wisconsin, is developing a youth confirmation course for members to have a "Life in Jesus" in the Word, in service, in the Cross, and in mission – connecting people to life in Jesus. This is a biblical curriculum for Christian growth and discipleship which is comprehensive in its scope. It designates the home as the central place for spiritual growth and development, supporting families in bringing up their children in the "nurture and disciplines of the Lord" (Eph. 6:4). It is the foundation for preparing people to express their Christian faith in the 21st Century. It gets beyond abstract truths and gets into fresh applications and realistic relations in the context of where people live.

The mission of the "Life in Jesus" course and curriculum is "to connect youth and families to life in Jesus." The central paradigm is to "offer a family-centered, church-supported, confirmation/discipleship ministry." The goals and objectives of the "Life in Jesus" courses and curriculum offer a self-regenerating cycle of beginning, living, and reaching out to connect people to God by:

1. Living their life in the Word that they will know Jesus fully first by completing adequate instruction in the Bible truths and catechisms and then regular personal devotions and journaling, regular prayer and a lifelong commitment to Bible study in small groups. "If you live in My Word, you are truly My disciples, and you will know the Truth and the Truth will set you free" (John 8:31-32);

2. Living in service that they will serve Jesus by serving others, providing time, abilities and money on the basis of spiritual gifts, being involved in church and community events and projects; live a servant life: "I, your Lord and Teacher, have washed your feet, now you must wash each other's feet. I've given you an example that you should follow" (John 13: 14-15);

3. Living under the Cross by dying to self and living in Jesus; developing a strong identity in Jesus and developing and modeling Christian character through an open and nurturing environment. "If anyone would come after Me, he must deny himself and take up his cross daily and follow Me" (Luke 9:23);

4. Living in mission and connecting others to life in Jesus, discerning and developing a lifestyle witness based on the Christian calling in Christ. "All authority in Heaven and on earth has been given to Me. Therefore, go and make disciples of all nations, baptizing them in the name of the Father and of the Son and of the Holy Spirit, teaching them to obey everything I have commanded you. And surely I am with you always, to the very end of the age" (Mat. 28:18-20).

Leaders, Leadership and Resources or Curriculum to Empower Members to Live in Jesus

The church leaders should build an environment in which the pastor, elders/deacons and education board can minister to the members so that in return all members can minister to each other as they are organized for faithful care of all members of the church. A healthy congregation will offer apprenticeship or sponsorship for all new members in the Christian faith. This is a way of welcoming, nurturing and supporting those who are new to the Christian faith. The spiritual leaders bear a responsibility for providing the rich soil in which individuals can grow and be nourished in all aspects of their lives.

First and foremost, the **Membership Standard of Ten Biblical Expectations** should be known by all members at a specific date after the

"Christian Life Development Process of Moving from Membership to Missions" has been adopted and incorporated into the congregation. This begins the massive move away from the "cathedral church" or "fortress church", which becomes a mass exodus from the institutional paradigm to the body of Christ model.

Of the 12 Pillars (quality characteristics and leading indicators) of a healthy church, Pillars 3,5,6,8 and 9 are to be mined and the resources to be tapped. The resources begin with some catechitical instruction, in which the basic truths of Scripture are taught in an atmosphere where new members can comprehend salvation in Christ Jesus and our living in Him in a world created by God with a living faith in the Triune God and a healthy lifestyle together with others. It is at this time of learning catechism truths (Course 101) in an effective instructional form that new members learn the membership standard of ten biblical expectations. Course 102 is the **Spiritual Travel Guide**, a 15-week interactive Bible study course for small groups, applying and relating Christian truths to life. Through Bible study, members learn or relearn all the basic doctrines of the Bible for a strong Christian faith and life in Jesus. It is a very practical review of Christian beliefs, which helps people to embrace Christ fully and to express their faith naturally.

Course 103 is **Experiencing God** (Broadman, by Henry Blackaby and Claude King) which is a small group interactive Bible study which helps people grow spiritually, applying the Scriptures to their lives actively and relating their faith to others in an effective manner. It has led many to greater spiritual growth. Any possibility of "decision theology" in the book should be placed into the context of God's flow of grace both in salvation and in sanctification by the power of the Holy Spirit.

Course 104 **Spiritual Fitness Exercise**, is a 10-week small group study which leads participants to weekly activities of daily devotions, reading a short chapter of a provocative book, witnessing, care-giving and tithing. Weekly, the small group gathers to share their experiences in their servant events and studies for building their own faith and for edifying others.

Course 105 GRASP Spiritual Gifts a Guide for Discovering God-given Uniqueness and Developing a Personal Mission Statement. This includes G – Groundings (Values), R – Roles, A – Abilities, S – Spiritual Gifts, P – Passions. Available from MOUNTAIN MOVERS INTERNATIONAL, 4000 Midway Road Suite 303, Carrollton TX 75007; 214-435-0753 whamit@aol.com

Pillar 5, INSPIRING/HIGH IMPACT GOD-EXALTING WORSHIP SERVICES, requires worship services to be offered for uplifting spiritual experiences in spirit and in truth. We need to know the difference between the changeless and the changing, between doctrine and substance on one hand, and communication considerations of culture, language and style on the other hand.

Pillar 6, MULTIPLIED SMALL GROUPS/INTENTIONAL DISCIPLE-MAKING/GROWING IN COMMUNITY is the basis of all biblical learning and life application of the Christian faith. Small groups were an integral part of the life of the 1st Century church, as spiritual growth of the people and churches was experienced through Christ-centered small group Bible studies. Primary resources for organizing small groups are **9 *Keys to Effective Small Group Leadership*** (Kingdom Publishers, Mansfield, Pa., Carl F. George), and ***The Small Group Book: The Practical Guide for Nurturing Christians and Building Churches*** (Baker, L.E. Galloway).

Pillar 8, LOVING RELATIONSHIPS is also involved in building healthy members.

Pillar 9, CENTRALITY OF GOD'S WORD/GOSPEL/GRACE is central to all proclaiming, preaching, teaching, and all that is said and done in membership development for First Base and all the other bases.

Base Two – Committed to Maturity (Teach/Train/Empower Members Through Regular Bible Study/Small Groups)

Growing in Christ
2.
EMPOWERING MATURITY

Goals:
Growing in Christ
Being discipled
Become a discipler

Resources:
1. 21st Century Disciples with a 1st Century Faith (201)
2. Walk Through the Bible (202)
3. Divine Dream (203)
4. Bethel Services (204)

Leaders:
Education Board

If a congregation ignores **Base 2, Empowering Members for Maturity**, it is hardly possible to be a healthy church with healthy members. The focus of Base 2 is on making healthy leaders who embrace the "Christian Life Development Process, Moving from Membership to Missions," with the goal to be a discipler and leader on the Pitcher's (Process Enabler's) Mound.

We have allowed most members to miss Second Base (committed to maturity), letting them go instead from the first step of membership to the

Third Base of ministry/service. The result is that service or involvement in ministry is sometimes exercised without adequate understanding of God's Word or spiritual maturity to perform effectively. Congregations will do well to adopt a policy that all those who will assume leadership positions will be active in Bible study and leadership development.

Base two involves spiritual growth through knowledge and faith as members are involved in discipling courses for maturity and a willingness to be mentored. The focus is on developing the inner life (heart/character) rather than mere knowledge and external actions and behavior. Small group Bible studies help people know and experience God. Prayer and spiritual disciplines are to be taught. Mentoring relationships are to be established. A goal is that all members are aware of God's promises and are willing to be what God wants them to be, guiding them to a healthy lifestyle.

The basic resource for Base Two is Course 201, **21st Century Disciples With a 1st Century Faith**, a 26-week interactive leaders Bible study which is a comprehensive course that summarizes all the basic doctrines of the Christian faith, applied and related to the context of the 21st Century. The topics for growing to maturity include living with God – the nature of God, how God reveals Himself and communicates to us – living with myself, living with my family and fellowmen, living with my resources, and living in the body of Christ and in the church.

Another resource is Course 202, **Walk Through the Bible**, which has informed and awakened many Christians to an active expression of their Christian faith in their daily lives. Course 203 is **Divine Drama**, and Course 204 is **Bethel Series** for those congregations which have experienced success in these courses.

Servant-mission events and trips should be a part of the discipling and mentoring process of Base Two, Empowering for Maturity. The curriculum for Pillar 6, **Small Groups**, should be continued and as the leadership courses such as the **21st Century Discipling** course are offered through discipling and mentoring classes, the discipled ones can become disciplers.

Leaders responsible for Base Two are the pastor, education board and discipled leaders. **ChristCare Groups** (growing out of Stephen Ministries) is a comprehensive system for leading and organizing small group ministries in churches.

Base Three – Commitment to Service and Servanthood (Enlist and Mobilize)

Serving Christ
3.
MOBILIZING MINISTRY

Goals:
Gifted to Serve
Ministers of God's grace
Care-givers

Resources:
1. Spiritual Gifts Bible Study (301)
2. Stephen Ministries (302)
3. Living without Slaveries/Support groups (303)
4. Christian Stewards–Confronted (304)
5. Big Step Forward in Faith (305)

Leaders:
Stewardship Board, Social Ministries

Commitment to ministry at third base means serving in some area of the church's ministries, being trained as an apprentice, being mentored, and then becoming a leader or teacher when appointed. Churches generally have a wide range of 20% to 30% active in service in the church – reaching 3rd base.

Basic to the third base commitment is that members discover and use their spiritual gifts (Eph 4:7). Having been empowered through discipling courses on second base, members should grow into ministries and tasks which match their grace-gifts. Part of this training strategy includes establishing ministry apprenticeships for leadership development though on-the-job mentoring. The congregation then plans enlarging ministry opportunities and creating new ministries.

Base Three is about discovering and using spiritual gifts, leading into service activities and various ministries. The goal is to have members recognize that they are gifted to serve, and that they are to be ministers of God's grace in every aspect of their lives. They are also to be care-givers to people in their circle of family, friends and neighbors who are hurting.

As they were empowered by the Second Base's discipling courses, Christian disciples are to go into ministries which match their grace-gifts. Some of it should be done through ministry apprenticeships by on the job mentoring.

Resources should begin with a specific Bible study course selected by the pastor and leaders on "**Spiritual Gifts**."

A basic course for all members (Course 303) is *Living Without Slaveries*. This is a 15-week interactive Bible study first to help hurting people with addictions, compulsions and obsessions, and second to train members who will be leaders to help the church organize support groups and to teach others this Bible study. This is part of the interactive Bible study curriculum for the second or third year of discipling, especially recruiting those who have the ability to be caregivers, and also those who are struggling with addictions, compulsions, and obsessions.

The suggested Course 302 is **Stephen Ministries**, (2045 Innerbelt Business Center Drive, St. Louis, MO 63114-5765; 314-428-2600; www.stephenministries.org). Stephen Ministries' Mission Statement is "to proclaim through word and deed the Gospel of Jesus Christ by nurturing, edifying, educating, and equipping the whole people of God who are called, gifted, and sent to be more effective servants who care for the needs of the whole person." Disciples are instructed for spiritual growth and trained in the skills necessary for caring ministry through 50 hours of training – plus ongoing supervision and continued education – in order to minister to people in crisis or need. Servitude is the basic goal of the training. Resource manuals and materials are offered for quality Christian care and ministry to people in crisis in many situations and conditions.

The other major responsibility of leaders in mobilizing members for ministry on Base Three is Christian stewardship and giving. Resources are **Pillar 2, GIFTS-ORIENTED SERVICE/MINISTRY,** and **Pillar 11, BIBLICAL FINANCIAL STEWARDSHIP**. Resources are: 1. *Christian Stewards Confronted and Committed* which is a basic resource for congregation stewardship committees and leaders in order to conduct an effective stewardship and giving educational program for all members; 2. *Big Step Forward in Faith* (Discipling/Stewardship Center, Waldo J. Werning), an 8-week series of both stewardship sermons and Bible studies together with other resources; 3. *New Beginnings – In Christian Living and Giving*, a 4-week stewardship/spiritual growth plan for congregations which include expository sermons and Bible studies and stewardship letters to members. Leaders for Base 3 Mobilizing for Ministry are the Stewardship Board and the Social Ministries Board.

Base Four – (Committed to Evangelism/Missions (Sharing Christ by Witnessing and Mission Outreach)

Sharing Christ
4.
MOBILIZING MISSIONS

Goals:
Making Christ known
Messengers of God's love

Resources:
1. The Way of Life (401)
2. Go and Tell (402)
3. Winning Friends for Christ (403)

Leaders:
Evangelism/Mission Board

The evangelism and mission leaders provide a program and approach in which a majority of the members may be effective in missions and evangelism – sharing the saving Gospel with all those with whom they come into contact, building relationships with those who are without Christ in order to share the Good News of the Gospel. Members are to be challenged to go beyond their comfort zone to be sent out into Christ's harvest field on servant and mission events locally, nationally and internationally. All eyes are to be open to the world harvest, and move across cultures.

A key evangelism resource is *The Way to Life* (Fairway Press or Discipling/Stewardship Center, Waldo J. Werning), which provides workshop training materials for witnessing and individual mentoring of members and new believers to share the saving Gospel with others.

Mission education programs should be offered so that members are informed about world missions and to get involved in the missions of their church. Members are to be encouraged and challenged to be involved in local servant events and mission opportunities, nationally and internationally. **Pillar 7, WITNESSING/ FRUITFUL EVANGELISM/MISSIONS** and **Pillar 10, MISSION AND VISION DRIVEN** are to be reviewed by leaders for more information, activities and resources.

Pitcher's Mound/Process Enablers Mound – Healthy Leaders for Healthy Churches and Healthy Members

---

Leading for Christ
P (Pitcher's Mound)
MOBILIZING LEADERSHIP

Goals:
Leading to Build a Helathy Church
Mentoring to Lead the Way

Resources:
1. 12 Pillars of a Healthy Church (501)
2. Natural Church Development (502)
3. God Says Move (503)
4. Purpose-Driven Church (504)
5. Paradigm Shift in the Church (505)
6. Maxwell, Partners in Prayer (506)

Leaders:
Pastors, Disciples

Empowering is an adjective which should always precede the word **leadership**. Empowerment gives leaders the training and the tools to use their grace-gifts as God directs. Empowerment gives them the ability to **mobilize** God's people for mission.

The pastor's leadership must focus on empowering and mobilizing God's people for mission. Leadership training focuses first on the pastoral office, then on the lay ministry. The pastoral function is to build a unified team which leads to a full-bodied fellowship of believers. The goal is to disciple leaders who bill build a healthy church.

Each congregation's leadership strategy should include the provision that all officers and leaders should not only be active in Bible studies, but also be involved in leadership courses, such as **12 Pillars of a Healthy Church, Natural Church Development, God Says Move – Go Where He Leads**, and **Purpose Driven Church**. A transition time of several years should be offered to all officers and leaders who are not participating in Bible studies and leadership courses. All Sunday School and Bible class teachers also should be involved in these leadership training courses.

There will be no healthy congregations unless there are healthy pastors and healthy leaders who disciple the members faithfully. Healthy leaders build healthy churches with healthy members. Church health comes from consistent study of God's Word and on-going leadership training courses, besides personal mentoring of individuals.

For developing the leadership training, Pillar 4, FUNCTIONAL STRUCTURES model is to be studied for the information and resources available for leadership development. Pillar 10, MISSION AND VISION-DRIVEN, reminds us to keep renewing our vision and mission statements consistent with the new insights God has given leaders for mission and ministry strategies.

Study courses which all leaders should read and study are:

1. Course 501, **12 Pillars of a Healthy Church** (Fairway Press or Discipline/Stewardship Center, Waldo J. Werning) provides not only the 8 quality characteristics and 4 leading indicators for a healthy church, but also offers the "Christian Life Development Process, Moving from Membership to Missions" grid for transforming a congregation to a Biblical Model to be a Great Commission Church.

2. Course 502, **Natural Church Development** (ChurchSmart Resources, Christian Schwarz) offers discoveries of world-wide research in 1000 congregations to learn the quality characteristics of a healthy church. Using the illustration of a barrel with staves to symbolize the quality characteristics, it is shown that the barrel can only hold water to the height of the lowest stave. Christian Schwarz demonstrates that a church can only grow as far as its "minimum factor."

3. Course 503, **God Says Move – Go Where He Leads** (Fairway Press, Waldo J. Werning) proposes the mission of God to be about moving and mapping for ministry and mission. Based upon the New Testament model, many barriers are identified as maintenance and institutional restrictions to Christ's mission. There is a sharp focus on the historic tension between Biblical doctrine and church practice. God's people must be mobile, coming and going, and gathering and scattering to reach everyone everywhere with the saving knowledge of Jesus Christ.

4. Course 504, **Purpose-Driven Church** (Zonnervan, Rick Warren) provides the foundation for a healthy church upon which are built its vision, objectives, goals, strategies and ministries. It is a gold mine for turning attenders into members and developing mature members and a vigorous church.

5. Course 506, **Partners in Prayer** (John Maxwell) provides both a book and video to give massive prayer support for the pastor and the church.

CHRISTIAN LIFE DEVELOPMENT PROCESS FOR MEMBERS AND LEADERS
MOVING FROM MEMBERSHIP TO MISSIONS
Transforming a Congregation to a Biblical Model

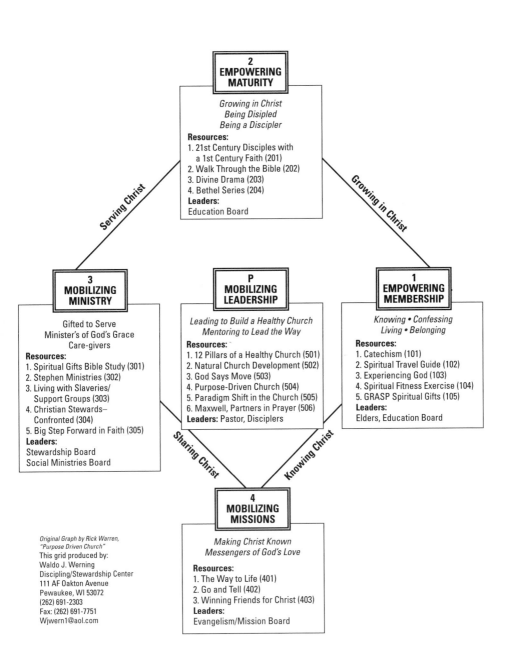

2
EMPOWERING
MATURITY

Growing in Christ
Being Disipled
Being a Discipler
Resources:
1. 21st Century Disciples with
   a 1st Century Faith (201)
2. Walk Through the Bible (202)
3. Divine Drama (203)
4. Bethel Series (204)
Leaders:
Education Board

Serving Christ

Growing in Christ

3
MOBILIZING
MINISTRY

Gifted to Serve
Minister's of God's Grace
Care-givers
Resources:
1. Spiritual Gifts Bible Study (301)
2. Stephen Ministries (302)
3. Living with Slaveries/
   Support Groups (303)
4. Christian Stewards–
   Confronted (304)
5. Big Step Forward in Faith (305)
Leaders:
Stewardship Board
Social Ministries Board

P
MOBILIZING
LEADERSHIP

Leading to Build a Healthy Church
Mentoring to Lead the Way
Resources:
1. 12 Pillars of a Healthy Church (501)
2. Natural Church Development (502)
3. God Says Move (503)
4. Purpose-Driven Church (504)
5. Paradigm Shift in the Church (505)
6. Maxwell, Partners in Prayer (506)
Leaders: Pastor, Disciplers

1
EMPOWERING
MEMBERSHIP

Knowing • Confessing
Living • Belonging
Resources:
1. Catechism (101)
2. Spiritual Travel Guide (102)
3. Experiencing God (103)
4. Spiritual Fitness Exercise (104)
5. GRASP Spiritual Gifts (105)
Leaders:
Elders, Education Board

Sharing Christ

Knowing Christ

4
MOBILIZING
MISSIONS

Making Christ Known
Messengers of God's Love

Resources:
1. The Way to Life (401)
2. Go and Tell (402)
3. Winning Friends for Christ (403)
Leaders:
Evangelism/Mission Board

Original Graph by Rick Warren,
"Purpose Driven Church"
This grid produced by:
Waldo J. Werning
Discipling/Stewardship Center
111 AF Oakton Avenue
Pewaukee, WI 53072
(262) 691-2303
Fax: (262) 691-7751
Wjwern1@aol.com

Who's on First, Second, Third, Home Base and Pitcher's Mound?

It will be important for church leaders to evaluate each member to learn whether he/she has grown beyond first base and, if so, whether he/she has passed second base or skipped it. A simple evaluation of where all the members are can be made in the following manner:

EVALUATION of total membership - how many are on each base?

1st base

   1) On base_____

   2) In the dugout or bleachers_____

2nd base _____

3rd base _____

Home base _____

Pitcher's mound _____

Recognizing what bases have been reached by the members of the congregation will help leaders minister and teach more effectively in order to become a healthy Christian community. The healthy church focuses on the disciple's relationship with Christ and the church. The ministry that takes place at each base stems from this important foundation. This approach helps us focus on disciples, the people Jesus called us to serve, and keeps us busy at our basic priority.

Empowering and mobilizing God's people for mission results from being strong in all 12 pillars. This happens when leaders shepherd all members to take them from base one to base two to base three to home base. This aids us to discover, develop, and deploy God's people as mature leaders and workers. It helps us to raise our ministries to their highest power and develop new ministries. Disciple-making is not completed until leaders have helped people become mature and enabled them to be reproducers themselves.

Healthy churches emphasize disciple-making as a spiritual dynamic. Healthy disciple-making churches are both inward-focused and outward-focused. They understand their challenge to build people – not just programs, buildings, and budgets. They know they exist to serve God by serving people. They influence more by their character and commitment to a Biblical process than by their programs. They will go the distance whether the roads are rough or not, taking the road less traveled. As they empower, they set the laity free and mobilize them to go where God leads.

Breakthrough leaders in healthy churches know that it starts and ends with them, and that influence is more important than control. They enhance spiritual growth and nurture fellowship, identify new leaders, strengthen Christian discipleship, and expand ministry opportunities.

Church health and results will be evaluated by Biblical principles for confession, life, worship, and practice, realistic administrative points of reference, how many members are in Bible study, how many are trained as leaders, and how many are actively involved in service, giving, evangelism, and mission.

Healthy churches recognize that making disciples is not an option. To them, the Great Commission is every individual's responsibility. They encourage a Great Commission lifestyle.

Leaders and members will hold themselves accountable to God and to each other to be shown trustworthy. "Let a man so consider us, as servants of Christ, and stewards of the mysteries of God. Moreover, it is required in stewards that one be found faithful" (1 Cor.4:2)

A Healthy Church is a LIFE-GIVING Church

In an August 1994 Conference in Denver, Ted Haggerd of Colorado Springs told of classifying healthy congregations with a strong spiritual character and qualities as Life-giving churches.[34] This challenged me to explore the Scriptures related to the Life-giving Jesus as the Bread of Life and the Water of Life, viewing the church as a fountain or river of Living Water. A Life-giving church has a full and complete menu of the Word and Gospel of Jesus Christ. God has called the church to be a spiritual pasture and grazing land where people can move and feed on the riches of His good land (Ez 34:14). *God Says Move* (pp. 198-199) gives a portrayal of the Life-giving church.

Priority of a Religion/Ritual/ Program-Giving Church	Priority of a Life-Giving Church
Religion/Rituals	Gospel/Conversion/Nurture
Justification	Justification-Sanctification
Programs	Process/Education/ Modeling/Mentoring
Prescribed Behavior	Relationships
Needs/Volunteers	Gifts Discovery and Use
Controlled by What's Expected (Legalism)	Controlled by God's Love (Grace)
Focus on Methods/Styles/Rules	Focus on Gospel/Substance
Maintenance	Mission
Budgets/Fundraising	First Fruit Proportionate Giving/Tithing
Controlled by the Institution, imprisoned by traditions	Freedom to be what God calls us to be
Corporate Style	Great Commission Style

Traditional church programs that are revised and tweaked regularly to update them for new challenges limit and restrict reaching the true potential because they are based on human vision of the past that are restrained by past experiences, imprisoned by traditions and controlled by institutional thinking. The program approach is a distraction from divine promises of miraculous growth, disruption from Biblical principles, and regular disappointments in failing to reach statistical goals. What emerges and follows is loss of energy and ultimately burn-out. Congregations which maintain program-centered activities usually are declining because of a wrong ministry focus as they fail to make the Great Commission and outreach mission as their priority.

Pastors of program-centered congregations could abandon 30% of in-basket matters and name 4-5 meetings they *must* attend, and miss all others. They serve struggling congregations which focus their attention and effort on themselves, being directed inwardly to conducting meetings and keeping statistics large enough to maintain the institution.

Life-giving churches have various ministries that focus their attention on the Great Commission and reaching the lost with the saving message of Jesus. They communicate in mission language keeping true to Biblical truths, while learning new ways to communicate them faithfully. Pastors of Life-giving churches are happy with the progress experienced by God's grace in nurturing the spiritual growth of God's people without expecting perfection. Their strategies focus on mission, not meetings, concentrating on spiritual development of the people, not on gaining numbers of members and church attenders.

Life-giving churches will experience this freedom to be what God calls them to be. Christians are revived and congregations are renewed as these churches pursue the vision and strategy of **12 *Pillars of a Healthy Church*, *Natural Church Development***, and adopt goals and strategies, as they use the resources, to take members to all four bases of Rick Warren's ballfield grid, and to take leaders to the pitcher's mound. The result is the multiplying and reproducing of believers, not just adding members. It empowers believers to become mobilized and engaged in the comprehensive, extensive, and all-embracing work Christ has given His church, putting them on a life-long journey of lively discipleship.

The goal of the Life-giving church is to make disciples and to empower and mobilize God's people for mission, while the religion-giving church seeks decisions and gaining of more church members – a difference between Christian discipleship and church membership. A Life-giving church seeks to encourage pure motives of service because of Christ's love, while the other comes off as duty.

Adopt a Planning Pyramid Which Begins with Clear Vision and Ends with Effective Ministry

How do we organize our strategy for ministry? Program-giving churches ordinarily look at their existing programs and try to bring some new insights for doing the work more effectively. The normal approach for most churches in developing their action plans is to focus on the various tasks of the congregation, emphasizing institutional needs. They assume that traditional practice has provided Biblical vision, objectives, goals and practices which need only to be carried out through planning meetings. These action plans are often badly distorted by beginning and remaining with traditional ministry without first adopting a Biblical strategy and map.

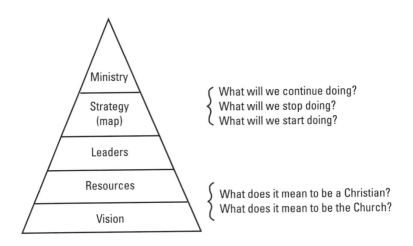

The planning pyramid shows that ministry is performed only after leaders have developed their vision, studied the resources, looked at the leadership situation, and then developed a strategy or map.

As we look at the planning pyramid and face various ministry responsibilities, the first step is to ask, "What is your purpose? What is the Biblical imperative? What is God's model?" Thus we begin by defining the goals and clarifying the vision. Then we move on to study the resources and leadership to develop strategies, which are the blue-print for our ministries.

The Biblical model or pyramid which we should follow, building layer upon layer, starts with the foundation and moves to the top, in the following manner:

1. VISION (General Map) Vision is gained from the Biblical blue-print and translates into objectives and goals in obedience to the Great Commission of Christ. Biblical vision views the church primarily as the body of Christ, not as an institution. It focuses on educating and

equipping the saints, worship, prayer, edifying, fellowship, service/giving/stewardship, and witnessing. Vision is developed from our Biblical understanding and commitment, followed by incorporating the details considered in the next steps, ending with strategy.

If we find it hard to have clear vision and objectives on which to build our ministry, some foundational questions must be considered. We should ask, *"What does it mean to be 'Christian'? What does it mean to be 'the church'?"* Leaders should persist in seeking answers to these questions until the group has reached full consensus.

2. RESOURCES. After the Biblical vision have been set, leaders look at available resources, which include people and their God-given gifts, abilities, time, and money. What has God given to make His mission possible? We identify our tools for ministry by recognizing what workers and supplies God has provided for the tasks.

3. LEADERS. The Biblical model lays great emphasis on the pastor, elders, and church leaders to lead the people where God wants them to go. Effective leaders are ones who have been discipled. They are ones who involve themselves in life-long Bible study, regularly participating in special educational opportunities and courses for gaining greater maturity. Qualified and trained leaders should be the standard requirement for candidates for church offices.

4. STRATEGY (Map). Strategy is the development of a master plan of education, evangelism, mission and stewardship (a spiritual map) to show the congregation where the leaders believe God wants them to go and to which they should respond. This is the blueprint and map which leaders develop and then consistently check to make certain that they pursue priorities in their ministry.

Notice the questions to be answered when we adopt our strategy or write our map, "What will we continue doing? What will we stop doing? What will we start doing?" The answering of these questions is an important step toward a more functional and aggressive ministry.

5. MINISTRY. The ministry plan of the congregation grows out of the first 4 steps of the pyramid: vision, resources, leaders, and strategy. This is the doing and living of the vision and Biblical pattern and the use of all the God-given resources. Under the leadership of the pastor and the church officers, vision is now translated from strategy into action without being disrupted by institutional and corporate barriers. Various ministries are planned to provide full service for all members of the congregation to reach the community and the world for Christ. Here the Word/Sacrament ministry is converted into purposeful activities by Christian priests in obedience to the will of God by His grace and the Holy Spirit's power.

The Transition from a Program-Giving to a Life-Giving Mission Church requires a Great Commission Congregation

The Great Commission Congregation is a multi-dimensional church, as it is defined, driven, developed and directed by the Word of God, not by its traditions, institutional requirements, or human expectations. [35]

The Great Commission Congregation is **defined** by God's Word and Christ's mission in the context of its own culture and community in relation to the entire world. It knows, understands, determines, specifies, communicates and makes clear its central nature, quality, purpose and distinguishing features, which defines what it is – its DNA.

The Great Commission Congregation is **driven** by the Gospel and motivated by Christ's love to be empowered, inspired and compelled by Jesus Christ, Who is the Sender, and Who provides the spiritual dynamic which guides the church as a mission movement. The power of the Holy Spirit is in the love, compassion, and rescue mission of Christ.

The Great Commission Congregation is **developed** by the Word through discipling by pastors and spiritual leaders, instructed through Bible study and leadership development to have its ministry formed, built and shaped through the means of grace. The same Word that brought the congregation into being, now develops it to expand and advance with a continuing state of effective mission-mindedness.

The Great Commission Congregation is **directed** by the Lord of the Church through the leaders for the discovery and use of their spiritual gifts. It carries out the mandate of the Great Commission as instructed by the will of the Sender, Jesus Christ, who regulates the tasks of the congregation by the Holy Spirit to open eyes to the harvest field, and aimed at the urgent task of discipling all people and reaching the lost with the saving Gospel of Jesus Christ in all cultures everywhere.

The Transition from a Program-Giving to a Life-Giving Mission Church requires a Great Commission Pastor

The focus of the congregation's ministry will not be on missions if the pastor's focus is not on missions. The pastor's ministry is not only to care for the individual and care for the church, but also to reach the non-churched. The pastor's as well as the congregation's strategy and map must include discipling believers and reaching non-believers.

When we think about the pastoral **office**, we must also deal in terms of **function**, which Paul certainly does. He writes more about pastoral service than with pastoral status, with the responsibilities and accountability more than the position. David S. Luecke in **New DESIGNS for Church LEADERSHIP** [36] shows from the Scriptures that pastoral ministry is more than being a shepherd, preaching, and administering the Sacraments. The word "pastor" comes from the Latin for shepherd, but a Biblical study shows that this pastor image can be challenged as incomplete.

Luecke explores the area of leader and administrator in today's context. A New Testament leader-analogy of **steward** (I Cor. 4:1-2) or **manager** (Luke 12:42) is a helpful identity.

The Scriptures reveal the basic theme of the pastor and church in **building** a house or in building the body of believers as a fellowship. Luecke outlines the work of pastors and church leaders as fellowship builders [37]. These are the builders: carpenter, contractor, and architect.

Paul called himself an "expert builder" (I Cor. 3:10), which could be understood as an architect. That's how he was leading. The basic analogy is the building function – fellowship building. In I Cor. 3:10-14, Paul had architectural concerns "for the right beginnings, the best materials, and sturdy design." He "expressed the overall vision for how a gathering of Christians should fit together in relation to each other, to God and to all people" (Eph. 2:19-22). His building commitment is shown in Eph. 4:12, where he says that the work of leaders is to "prepare God's people for works of service, for the building of the body of Christ." The design for building a fellowship is best seen in verse 16: "From Him (Christ) the whole body, joined and held together by every supporting ligament, grows and builds itself up in love, as each part does its work."

Paul shows himself to be a contractor in 2 Cor. 10:8 and 13:10, telling that he wanted to help the Corinthian Christians, not hurt them, to build them up rather than pull them down. The contractor emphasis is evident in 1 Cor. 12 in which the building theme refers to the development of the body of Christ, seeking the unity of the Body amidst diversity of spiritual gifts. The Book of Acts shows Paul at work with hands-on fellowship building: healer (Acts 14:8-10); strengthening the various churches (14:22; 15:21); exhorting the house group in Philippians (15:40); teaching daily in the lecture hall of Tyrannus (18:9). Paul makes little use of the shepherd image in his writings.

Peter also refers to what God is doing in His Church, which pastors and congregations need to recognize. He says, "...You also, like living stones, are being built (as a fellowship) into a spiritual house, to be a holy priesthood..." (1 Pet. 2:4-5). Peter shows that the Christian mission is not finished when people become living stones through a church's ministry of Word and Sacrament, but these new stones must now be put together to become a household. The work of pastors and leaders is to make certain that Christians are not inactive or passive stones, but lively stones. The end result of the pastoral function is the building of a full-bodied fellowship of believers.

The Bible divides the tasks of the pastor into various classifications: Feed the flock of God and take oversight of the congregation (1 Peter 5:2); the pastor is to govern diligently and work faithfully (Rom. 12:8; 1 Thes.

5:12; 1 Thes. 5:17); he is to preach, teach, disciple, be a fellowship builder, be a Great Commission pastor, and administer the spiritual affairs of the congregation. His authority under Christ is conferred by God through the congregation, which holds the priesthood power.

The Biblical pattern of pastoral leadership is complex. John Finney in his book, **Understanding Leadership**[38] groups pastoral leadership around four words: Servant, Shepherd, Steward, Episkopos (bishop, someone who watches over).[39] Finney's pattern of pastoral leadership deals with care for the individual and care for the church, to which we must add care for the non-believers as a Great Commission pastor (Matt.28: 18-20). As you look at the grid which follows, each word serves as a focus for Biblical ideas and titles. They are interlocking circles, each word and ministry function is a continuum stretching from care for each person to concern for the corporate whole to discipling members and reaching the lost. Pastoral leadership forces hard decisions which come from the tensions between various roles.

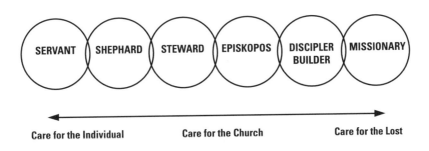

As a servant of God and a steward of the mysteries of God, the pastor is a servant of God's people in the church and the non-believers in the world. Mark 10:43-45 presents the servant nature of the Christian faith that, like Christ the pastor "did not come to be served, but to serve." The care for the whole church and for non-believers does not allow the pastor to get side-tracked by trying to fulfill the expectations of all members or to be a servant to manipulators. With Christ, the pastor is one who is among the people as one who serves. (Lk. 22:27)

The role of the pastor as shepherd is ordinarily most familiar to us as a traditional function, but as the Scriptures show, there are other functions which call for the care of the entire church and for reaching the unchurched as discipler and as missionary.

The steward is the main figure in a number of parables told by Jesus, showing the characteristics of faithfulness, management skills, and the ability to be responsible for those for whom he is accountable. Christian leaders are described as "stewards of the mysteries of God" (1 Cor. 4:1). Sometimes the pastor/steward guides by a prophetic voice in order to set the vision of God before the people.

As episkopos or overseer, the pastor is to guide the church so that there is adequate coordination and discipline to experience unity in the life of the congregation. The pastor is to watch over the members of the body of Christ so that all function effectively according to the gifts which Christ has given them. The pastor is obligated to proclaim the Word of God in its full truth and purity, to administer the Sacraments faithfully, and to perform his other duties in accordance with God's will.

As we look at the **Christian Life Development Process** grid which shows members moving from membership to maturity, to ministry, to missions, and some to be discipled as leaders, we need to recognize that this does not happen because the pastor conducts or attends numerous meetings, but because he has become a discipler and a missionary, as well as shepherd of the flock. Such a Great Commission pastor will guide his congregation to transition from being program-giving to Life-giving. The pastor, leaders and members will be a united body of Christ responding to Jesus' invitation to be active in the Great Commission by making disciples. Spiritual development occurs rapidly in people who are in ministry and mission.

Quiet Conversations by Alan C. Klaas and Cheryl D. Klaas [40] offers valuable insignts for pastors to avoid burn-out and near burn-out by changing from maintenance, programatic, and corporate ministry to mission, life-giving, relational ministry. A way out of the deadening spiral of tension, conflict, and relocation is offered to be replaced by leadership development training and a formal lay mobilization system. Describing the nature and behavior of pastors and congregations experiencing difficulties, the book gives a practical, understandable guide to a healthier and more faithful life for pastors and their congregations.

Changing to a Grace, Body of Christ Paradigm – Introducing and Changing to the Biblical Paradigm Without a Battle

The debate over the church as an organism contrasted to an organization, of an institution or the body of Christ, has been active for most of 2000 years. The fact is that any deviation to the left or the right – to the static or dynamic – and a failure to have a balanced approach of being *in* the world without being *of* the world is a faulty one.

First, some need to stop fighting against something, but accept the Biblical view. It may take different forms, but grace theology will prevail, and the Biblical boundaries will be kept. The bipolar thought model (static and dynamic poles) with the acceptance of *12 Pillars of a Healthy Church* and leading all members to all four bases – and some as leaders to the pitcher's mound – of the ballfield is a lifelong journey which should begin now.

Christian Schwarz in his book, *The Threefold Art of Experiencing God*

(ChurchSmart), tells how to change paradigms without manipulation: "1. Never try to change another person's paradigm. 2. Try to learn from your opponents. 3. Create a climate where change can easily happen. 4. Welcome conflicts between paradigms. 5. Instead of struggling against heresies, strengthen the opposing poles." [41]

Schwarz makes an important observation that all this happens by the guidance of the Holy Spirit, and that we need a balanced view of the Triune God, avoiding syncretism, dogmatism, and spiritualism. While presenting them in human terms, the Principles which I have shared, together with those of Christian Schwarz and Rick Warren, have their source in the Bible.

We are making a loud cry not to conduct church as though it is a religious museum of past practices, programs, ancient cultural styles, or traditional and institutional forms, but the lively, organic body of Christ. This is not a flight into pragmatism, but an expedition – and hopefully a mass migration – back to the essence of the 1st Century Church.

Addressing the possibility of discouragement, Rick Warren states, "Don't worry about the growth of your church. Focus on the purposes of your church." Paul says "Let us not become weary in doing good, for at the proper time we will reap a harvest if we do not give up" (Gal. 6:9). It begins with being a purpose-driven person. What is required is a person who truly believes and trusts God – one who does not hold to human and institutional addition, but to the Holy Spirit's multiplication. We are not looking for a better version of the past, but rather improvements of the nature and conditions of church life in the present.

As traditional, mechanistic structures and procedures are replaced with principles of organic forms of organization, the church will more easily reflect the vitality of the church displayed in Ephesians 4. This is not rooted in administrative techniques, organizational theory, but in seeking the Kingdom of God first. We can obtain church health by God's grace. It's His church, not ours.

"Carpe Diem!" "Seize the Day!"

Those who seize the day will go back to Biblical basics with theologically rich messages and simple and practical methods to communicate that Word. Courageous leaders will be truth-tellers and not hide reality from the people. They are not fearful, but are apologists for the faith of the Fathers. They do not squander their Gospel freedom and prosperity. Their speech matches the problem to be solved. They teach Biblical theology, direct toward creative and changing methods, in the freedom of the Gospel, are deeply involved in the mission context, and are engaged with the people in constant renewal of the church.

Those who "seize the day" ask, "What is our policy?" and answer, "We are waging war against everything that is tainted with sin and that has been humanly contrived!" When they are asked, "What is our aim?" they proclaim, "By God's grace we will gain victory in Christ and for Christ!" When they are asked, "What is our strategy?" they answer, "We aim to be the kind of church God wants us to be! Our text is the Bible, not institutional manuals!"

Stuart Briscoe wrote a small pamphlet many years ago, which incorporated four reasons why Christian leaders can be victorious in leading the church to be the Church of the Lord Jesus Christ. He wrote:

"1. It's easy." Jesus promises victory that the gates of hell would not prevail against the church.

"2. It's difficult." It's difficult because of all the human factors, living with many people who have different views and paradigms, ones who stand for institutional loyalty over against Biblical faithfulness.

"3. It's impossible." How can Gideon's 300 win over the multiplied thousands of the enemy? In view of all the historical and present problems which the church has inherited, and some of the negative factors which control the life of the church, how can we gain victory over the devil, the world, and our sinful flesh? It's impossible.

"4. It's exciting." It's exciting because Christ has overcome the world and defeated Satan. His victory now is ours, and that's exciting! It's not a dream world, but it's the reality of God's grace and the Holy Spirit's power in the Gospel, in our lives in Jesus.

God's grace will cause us to be servants of Christ who know what it is to love God with all our minds, as well as our hearts, souls, and bodies. With ears of faith we hear the summons to know, love, and obey God for the extension of Christ's Kingdom to God's glory by the power of the Holy Spirit.

It took Israel forty years to make an eleven day trip. An institutional wilderness journey will not get us from here to "there." Only as we set our minds on things above (Col. 3:1-2), will eyes of faith give us vision to avoid the desert and wilderness of organizational confusion, not looking where we came from, but looking at the Word. Some will stop going around the same mountain of legalism over and over, while others will stop swimming in the sea of undefined freedom of the Gospel.

Courageous Christians will heed the word of Joshua, "Now therefore, arise, go over this Jordan, you and all this people, to the land which I am giving to them..." (Josh. 1:2). We will not get tired of doing the right thing: "Let us not grow weary while doing good, for in due season we shall reap if we do not lose heart" (Gal. 6:9)

Yes, it is exciting to be on a lifelong journey of lively discipleship, being first-class pastors, teachers, spiritual leaders, care givers and personal witnesses in a healthy church. It is exciting to reach a higher plateau of Word and Sacrament ministry with healthy leaders and healthy members to be a healthy church.

As a pastor and a spiritual leader, you have the *call* to lead. Do you have the *heart* to lead the church on a clear and compelling spiritual strategic journey? Are you one who is ready to make a mutual agreement with many other faithful leaders to measure church transformation one congregation at a time, beginning with yours?

Master Mission Statement for a Life-Giving Church and a Center for Missionary Formation

---

**Life-Giving Church
Center for Missionary Formation
(Church)
(City, State)**

Master Mission/Ministry Statement

I.   Our Mission: To establish a Great Commission passion in the local church.

II. Our Strategy: To assist our leaders to be functional and our congregation healthy through leadership training, mentoring, and Biblical resources for intensive nurture/educational activities.

III. We are committed to:

1. Obedience to the Great Commission by men, women, youth, and children, beginning with empowering and mobilizing leaders as a strategic way to have this accomplished;

2. Encouraging members to see themselves as part of the body of Christ in that place, to reach all the lost and serve hurting people through various ministries of the Gospel;

3. Maintaining ministry that revolves around Great Commission priorities, believing that Paul, like Jesus, not only gave us the mandate, but also modeled the method of ministry through his life (Matt 28:18-20; Eph 4:12-16; 2 Tim 2:2);

4. Training leaders in "discipling," centering on "every member a Bible student";

5. Making our congregation a Life-giving Church and Center for Missionary Formation by equipping all believers to be faithful witnesses of Jesus, teaching "every member to be a missionary";

6. Encouraging our pastor(s) and lay leaders to expect miracles in their ministries to the glory of Jesus Christ, that the congregation may be a healthy Life-giving Church.

IV. Our vision is to work together to share Christ's love passionately to develop a healthy church with 12 pillars of eight quality characteristics and four leading indicators which empowers and mobilizes God's people for mission.

APPENDICES
Several Planning Forms for Strategizing

OUR NEW GOALS AND STRATEGY

Our goal for _____ (area of parish responsibility)

1. Current situation: Where are we? What are the issues? What are the strengths and weaknesses?

2. Goal: State your goal, based on the facts discovered from the previous question and on scriptural objectives – a goal that is attainable, measurable, and challenging.

3. Alternative methods to reach the goal: Name all the alternatives of how you can grasp the opportunities, and then select the one that will best help you reach your goal.

4. Roadblocks: List all the obstacles you face in reaching this goal.

5. Short-range and long-range goals: Set dates for measuring the effectiveness of your strategy.

   A. State what you want accomplished in one year, by God's grace (give the date). _____

   B. State what you want accomplished in five years, by God's grace (give the date). _____

6. Develop your strategy: List all the steps required to carry out your ministries to achieve your goals – what you believe God wants you to accomplish.

   A. What are the resources available to pursue your goals, including people resources?

7. All this can be accomplished if we _____
   (Give as many answers as possible to finish this statement as you discuss prayerfully.)

TAKING ACTION...A WORKING GUIDE

(List all the steps required to carry out your plans to achieve your goals – what you believe God wants you to accomplish. Enlarge the following graph on a sheet of paper, and fill in the columns.)

Activity to be Done	Who Will Do It	Where and When	How- Resources	Budget Needs	Who Evaluates	Completed Check List

A SOCIAL MINISTRIES PROFILE OF YOUR PARISH

(Determine how many members fit each of the following categories, and then decide what ministries you have or need to develop in order to minister effectively to them.)

Widows   _____

Widowers   _____

Divorcees   _____

One-Parent Families:
   Male   _____

     Children at Home   _____

     Female   _____

     Children at Home   _____

Unemployed Heads of Families   _____

Employed Married Women   _____

With Children at Home   _____

Retired Men   _____

Retired Women   _____

Substandard Homes   _____

Families on Welfare   _____

Mentally Disadvantaged   _____

Physically Disadvantaged   _____

Non-Institutional Shut-Ins:
   Men   _____

     Women   _____

Institutionalized Shut-Ins:
    Nursing Homes   _____

    Hospitals for Disadvantaged

Known Alcoholics:
    Men   _____

    Women   _____

Baptized Members:
    Men   _____

    Women

    Children   _____

Communicant Members:
    Men   _____

    Women   _____

    Youth   _____

    Families   _____

ENDNOTES

[1] George Barna, **The Second Coming of the Church** (Nashville: Word Publishing, 1998, p. 8). All rights reserved.

[2] Barna, p. 9.

[3] "Growing Churches Conference," August 7-10, 1998, in Schaumberg, IL.

[4] Barna, p. 10.

[5] Barna, p. 1.

[6] George Barna, **The Barna Report, What Americans Believe** (Ventura, CA: Regal Books, 1991), p. 184.

[7] Robert N. Nash, Jr., an **8-Track Church in a CD World** (Macon, GA: Smyth & Helwys, 1997), p. 116.

[8] Reprinted from **The Once and Future Church: Reinventing the Congregation for a New Mission Frontier** by Loren Mead (AL129) with permission from the Alban Institute, Inc., 7315 Wisconsin Avenue, Suite 1250W, Bethesda, MD 20814-3211. Copyright 1991. All rights reserved.

[9] Leonard Sweet, **FaithQuakes** (Nashville: Abingdon Press, 1994), p. 170. Used by permission.

[10] Rick Warren, **The Purpose Driven Church** (Grand Rapids: Zondervan Publishing House, 1995).

[11] **The Lay-Driven Church**, by Melvin J. Steinbron (Regal Books, Ventura, CA 93003), p. 24. Used by permission.

[12] Christian E. Schwarz, **Natural Church Development** (St. Charles, IL: ChurchSmart Resources, 1996). ChurchSmart books and materials are available at 3830 Ohio Ave., St. Charles, IL 60174; phone: 1-800-253-4276; fax: 1-630-443-7929; e-mail: ChurchSmart@compuserve.com.

[13] **The Lay-Driven Church**, by Melvin J. Steinbron (Regal Books, Ventura, CA 93003), p. 59. Used by permission. Steinbron adds, in his footnote, "These Biblical references are for those who wish to study this part of Paul's life and ministry: father (1 Cor. 4:15; 1 Tim. 1:2); apostle (Rom. 1:1; 1 Cor. 15:9-10); leader (Acts 20:13-38); authority (1 Cor. 11:17-34); example (1 Cor. 4:16; 1 Thess. 1:6);

equal (1 Cor. 5:18-21; Phil. 4:3; 1 Thess. 3:2; Philem. 24); corrected (1 Cor. 5:1-5; Phil. 4:2); advised (1 Tim. 2:1-6; 2 Tim. 2:14-19); persuaded (Acts 17:16-34); exhorted (1 Tim. 1:3-7); compromised (Acts 16:3); suffered (Phil. 1:12-14; 4:10-13); adapted (1 Cor. 9:22); servant (Rom. 1:1; 1 Cor. 3:5; 4:1); sinner (Rom. 7:14-24; 1 Tim. 1:15-16); least apostle (1 Cor. 15:9)."

[14] George Barna, *The Second Coming of the Church* (Nashville: Word Publishing, 1998, pps. 130, 131). All rights reserved.

[15] *Putting an End to Worship Wars*, Elmer Towns (Nashville, TN: Broadman & Holman Publishers, 1997). Used by permission.

[16] Stephen Ministries, 8016 Dale, St. Louis, Missouri 63117-1449.

[17] Telecare Ministry Ev. Dpt., LCMS (314) 965-9000.

[18] Vallet and Zech: *The Mainline Churches' Funding Crisis* (William B. Eerdmans, 1995), pps. 146, 160.

[19] Christian Schwarz, pps. 103ff.

[20] David J. Hesselgrave, *Planting Churches Cross-Culturally: A Guide for Home and Foreign Missions* (Grand Rapids: Baker Bock House, 1980).

[21] Hesselgrave, pps. 61-63.

[22] Dr. Ray W. Ellis, in his article, "The Holy Spirit and Church Revitalization," in the book, *Church Revitalization, Getting Ready for the 21st Century* (published by Evangelism and Home Missions Association of the National Association of Evangelicals, September 1997).

[23] Christian Schwarz, pps. 103ff

[24] Christian Schwarz, p. 126

[24A] Illustration taken from *The Purpose-Driven™ Church* by Rick Warren, Copyright 1995 by Rick Warren. Used by permission of Zondervan Publishing House.

[25] Warren, pps. 15-17

[26] Warren, p. 28

[27] Warren, p. 30

[28] Warren, p. 32

[29] Warren, p. 60

[30] Warren, p. 61

[31] Warren, p. 87

[32] Warren, p. 117

[33] Rick Warren ballpark

[34] Ted Haggard has written a book, **The Lifegiving Church** (Ventura, CA: Regal Books, 1998), which offers foundations for Life-giving ministry based on the choice in Eden between the tree of Life (innocence, the gifts of the Spirit and anointing), and the tree of knowledge of good and evil (blame, condemnation and judgment). He reminds readers that our power is in the Spirit, not in the flesh. He tells of relationships which empower, for multiplication, importation, integration and demonstration of life.

[35] These paragraphs were developed from notes provided by Wilbert J. Sohn's on "The Dimentions of a Mission Congregation"

[36] David S. Luecke   **NEW DESIGNS for Church LEADERSHIP** (Fellowship Ministries, 6202 S. Maple Street, Tempe, AZ 85283

[37] Luecke, p. 26-40

[38] John Finney, **Understanding Leadership** (London, Daybreak,), Darton, Longmann, Todd LTD., 89 Lilly Road, London SW6 IUD England

[39] A full explanation of Finney's leadership grid is found in **God Say's Move – Go Where He Leads**, pgs. 173-175

[40] Alan C. Klaas, Cherly D. Klaas: **Quiet Conversations** (Mission Growth Publications, Kansas City, MO 2000)

[41] Schwarz, (**The Threefold Art of Experiencing God**, pps. 28-29)

COMMENDATIONS
FROM MISSION LEADERS

"12 Pillars of a Healthy Church takes the church health paradigm beyond a simplistic emphasis on inward renewal by restoring the outward focus on reaching the lost. Werning's four leading indicators – God's Word, Mission, Stewardship, Church Planting – are must reading."

> Dr. Gary L. McIntosh
> Professor, Talbot School of Theology

"Dr. Werning has provided a powerful challenge to get back to basics. The book has a strong Biblical base with lots of practical helps. He encourages churches to be Biblically based while at the same time culturally relevant. A solid help for any church that wants to grow and be a missional church."

> Rev. Hugh G. Townsend
> Associational Strategy Development Coordinator
> North American Mission Board
> Southern Baptist Convention

"In his book, 12 Pillars of a Healthy Church, Dr. Werning has not only given us the advantage of his years of knowledge and experience, but has addressed the key areas that can't be ignored by anyone wishing to build a church that ministers to itself and its community. I recommend it as a must to read."

> Dr. Larry Gilbert
> Church Growth Institute
> Forest, Virginia

"This is a critical moment in the history of the Christian Church. Many local churches are at a crossroads, and the decisions leaders will make in the next few years will determine the destiny of their congregation. Waldo Werning has clearly focused on health and vitality – issues at the epicenter for discipleship and mission. As he does so well, Dr. Werning has provided practical 'handles' to translate Biblical principles into action that God can use to revitalize the Church."

> Dr. Kent R. Hunter
> Church Doctor Ministries
> Corunna, IN

"In the introduction to 12 Pillars of a Healthy Church, Dr. Waldo Werning promised that he would take the reader past information and inspiration to application, that is, action! He delivers on that promise as he unfolds eight quality characteristics and four leading indicators of healthy churches. He does it in a clear, straight-forward manner that continually points to the grace of God as the empowering force for becoming a healthier church. The payoff in applying the insights contained in this book will be the growing of 'Life-giving churches' that make disciples who, in turn, make more disciples! The 'Realty Checks' at the end of each of the 12 pillars help the reader to focus on the heart of the issues. Werning's acquaintance with current research and his numerous years of experience as a church consultant are evident as he closes his book with a sense of hope for pastors and other church leaders, by highlighting a number of helpful resources and manageable action steps for developing a master strategy for becoming a healthier church!"

> Rev. Larry Reinhart
> Stewardship Counselor
> Board for Congregational Services
> The Lutheran Church-Missouri Synod

"Werning gives insightful church growth principles on leading a congregation through transition to be a healthier church. Pastors desiring theirs to become a Life-giving church will want to read this book."

> Dr. Ray Ellis
> President, American Society for Church Growth
> Senior Pastor, Willow Vale Community Church, CA

"When I grow up, I still want to think about 'doing church' the way Waldo Werning thinks about doing church. Waldo demonstrates powerful insights as he examines the dynamics of effective ministry in his book, 12 Pillars of a Healthy Church. Waldo correctly understands that the church is not the mission - it is established by God to accomplish the mission. In a practical and logical way, Waldo demonstrates what godly leaders have always known: 'God's work done in God's way will never lack God's supply!' I commend 12 Pillars of a Healthy Church to those enjoying God's blessings in ministry. It will provide a great opportunity for review and reflection. I especially recommend 12 Pillars of a Healthy Church to those who are frustrated with their ministries and are looking for insights that will help them understand important principles of health. Not every church will grow in dynamic ways, but every church should be a healthy place for Christians to gather and experience God's grace."

> Rev. Stephen Hower
> St. John's Lutheran Church, Ellisville, MO
> Founder, Association of Courageous Churches

"This book adds four additional crucial insightful steps beyond Natural Growth Development's eight essentials in a healthy church. A must-read for those interested in spiritual development as well as congregational growth."

Dr. Marlin Mull
General Director, Evangelism and Church Growth
The Wesleyan Church

"For the diligent pastor or leadership team, Waldo Werning's approach provides an effective path to increased fruitfulness. His minimum, moderate and maximum level assignments are particularly helpful."

Dr. R. Daniel Reeves
Past President
American Society for Church Growth

"Werning focuses on 12 foundational pillars of the healthy, Biblical church. He points out that, as God gives people an integrated physical life through the arteries and pulmonary system, so the body of Christ must embrace integrated, health-giving Word and Sacrament values. He calls for a shift from boards, committees, programs and meetings to a Scriptural study of the Biblically integrated life that triggers the quality characteristics of Christian witness and outreach. Werning believes this can best be done in small fellowship groups. He contends that, as the individual parts/pillars are strengthened and integrated, the whole church gets healthier."

Dr. Eugene W. Bunkowske
Graduate Professor of Missions and
 Supervisor of the Doctor of Missiology Program
Concordia Theological Seminary
Fort Wayne, Indiana

"When you understand the Bible, churches, and Natural Church Development, you have a formula for growing a healthy, vibrant church. Waldo Werning brings his keen insights and years of experience to those issues in 12 Pillars of a Healthy Church. Pastors in churches of all sizes and denominations will benefit from reading this book."

Dr. Robert E. Logan
Church Resources Ministry
Fullerton, CA

Contact us:
Discipling/Stewardship Center
Dr. Waldo J. Werning, Director
111 AF Oakton Avenue
Pewaukee, WI 53072
Phone/Fax: (262) 691-7751
e-mail: wjwern1@aol.com

Visit us at our website:
www.healthychurch.com